Still a Bit of Snap in the Celery

Still a Bit of Snap in the Celery

or K.B.O.

MARCUS BERKMANN

abacus
books

ABACUS

First published in Great Britain in 2023 by Abacus

1 3 5 7 9 10 8 6 4 2

A CIP catalogue record for this book
is available from the British Library.

ISBN 978-0-349-14548-8

Typeset in Times by M Rules
Printed and bound in Great Britain by
Clays Ltd, Elcograf S.p.A.

Papers used by Abacus are from well-managed forests
and other responsible sources.

Abacus
An imprint of
Little, Brown Book Group
Carmelite House
50 Victoria Embankment
London EC4Y 0DZ

An Hachette UK Company
www.hachette.co.uk

www.littlebrown.co.uk

To the fallen, the ones that didn't make it:
Kate Saunders, Esther Kaposi, Brian
Warr, Matthew Burrows, Bill Saunders,
Sarah Parker, Alan Dewhurst . . .

Contents

Introduction

Entering your sixties brings with it a warm and fuzzy
feeling of freedom through redundancy, through
obsolescence, through living outside of the conversation
and forever existing on the wrong end of the stick.

Nick Cave
The Red Hand Files

Back at the beginning of 2020, before Covid struck, we had
a kitchen put in.

(I should probably emphasise that we are not the sort of
people who idly, even casually, have kitchens put in. My
mother had inherited some money, and was so appalled by
our kitchen, which had remained unchanged for more than
thirty years, that she told us she wanted to buy us a new one.
We said yes, with grace and no little gratitude.)

The whole operation would take between three and four
weeks, and we were advised to move out for the duration. As
it happens, my partner Polly and my son James spent most, if
not all, of that time in the flat, breathing in copious quantities

of dust and shortening each of their lives by several decades. But I hit the road, and went off to visit some of my friends outside London that I hadn't seen for some time, in one or two cases years, and whom I had never previously seen in their natural habitat. A working holiday, I told these friends. I won't stay more than three days in any one place, because no guest ever should, and I am close to deadline on a book I'm writing, so you'll hardly see me. Have laptop, will travel.

Those three and a half weeks were one of the most fascinating experiences of my life. I learned so much about myself and about my friends (who, in all cases, I thought I knew pretty well) that I am anxious to do it again, go and see different people, maybe some of the same ones, go out and learn more. Next time I won't do it in January, because it was bloody cold everywhere, occasionally wet and often rather bleak. England in winter isn't for exploring; it's for staying inside, drinking tea and reading books.

As it happens, all the people I visited, except one couple, were about my age or a little older. I was born in July 1960, so at the time of my tour I was fifty-nine, with a prominent birthday on the horizon. In January I was trying my hardest not to think of this prominent birthday, but visiting people who had already passed through that terrifying threshold was actually a glimpse, not so much into the future but into different sorts of present that none of us could quite escape. One man (single, big house) was cheerful but lonely; one couple were missing their sons, who had all grown up and moved out; another couple told me they slept a lot, and they did, a hell of a lot; a third couple had the toughest job of all, looking after their granddaughters, aged seven and eight, because their rackety daughter couldn't look after them herself for drug-related reasons. Everywhere I went there was a slight undertow of sadness. Not terrible misery, because we are all British and we make the best of what we have, but a tinge of disappointment, of this-is-where-we-have-ended-up, of stoical acceptance of less than ideal circumstances. In the past we had our youth and the promise of what was coming next. Now our youth has vanished and what is coming next you really don't want to think about. We have made decisions, some of them ill-considered, others downright foolish, and now we have no choice but to live with the consequences of these decisions. So we do. It's not ideal.

The thing is, we're not old. We are fit (to an extent), we have all our marbles (at least for now) and our faces, some harder than before, some softer, tell the stories of our lives. When I was young I thought remarkably little of sixty-year-olds, mainly because I thought almost entirely of myself. Now I'm sixty other people matter much more to me, and the fragility of our lives, the knowledge that things may suddenly go wrong in a way that can never be put right, gives those lives a piquant new flavour. In Britain, relatively few people die in their fifties, but in their sixties they start keeling over in droves. I have three very good friends who were all born within six weeks of each other in 1949. (They are all in my pub quiz team, as it happens.) One of them, Chris, got a nasty cancer and died in early 2016, aged sixty-six. The other two, Patrick and Alan, are both fit and healthy and functional. Either of them could easily live another quarter-century. I myself am planning to live well beyond the age of a hundred, mainly to annoy people. When you are fifty, death is still freakish. When your friends die young, it's a shock and a surprise. When you are sixty it seems reasonable to assume that quite a lot of us won't be here in ten years' time. We don't know who, but we each hope it won't be us, and that we will still be here to see them off. When your friends die old, it's still a shock, but it's no longer a surprise.

About a decade ago I wrote *A Shed of One's Own*, a meditation (with jokes) on male middle age. At the age of fifty I had what I thought was the mother and father of all midlife crises, which turned out to be a perfectly ordinary, even boring, midlife crisis, and *Shed* was the result. I haven't re-read it since, because I have no strong wish to relive what I remember as particularly grim days. If you write autobiographically tinged non-fiction as I do, each book represents who you were when you wrote it, and if you can find the courage to re-read it later you will realise how much you and the world have changed in the years since. Whenever I look at *Rain Men*, my first book, which was about village cricket, I love the energy, the rage, the effervescence, the sheer bagginess of it, and recognise very little of what currently constitutes my life or my personality. I think a lot of us think of ourselves as serenely unchanging, as beacons of consistency in an uncertain world. Writers know otherwise, as do musicians, and artists of every stripe. You look at your early work and shudder, even if it was, objectively, so much fresher and more energetic than your later, more technically adept work. So this book doesn't dwell on what was then, because that has gone, for ever. Instead it seeks to describe what is now, when we are no longer young, but not yet old. We are somewhere in the middle, and even the term 'middle-aged' doesn't quite do it justice, because whippersnappers of forty-five could justifiably use that word to describe themselves. And 'late middle-aged' just sounds like a euphemism or, worse, a squeaky little genteelism, like saying you live in west West Hampstead when you really live in Cricklewood.

So Richard, my publisher and friend who is a year younger than me (but for god's sake don't tell his bosses because they will try to 'retire' him), and I coined the phrase 'young/old' to describe our current state. (That was actually the working title of this book.) We are far too old to be young, but we are also too young to be properly old. I still have all my hair and all but two of my teeth, but I have bags under my eyes you could carry the shopping in. Swings and roundabouts, swings and roundabouts. Not that we could go on either any more, as all that fast movement up and down and round and round would make us vomit, pass out or possibly die.

My friend Adrian, who is about nine months older than me, rejected the idea for this book out of hand. 'What do you mean, young/old? We're just old.' He said this while sitting in the pavilion at Lord's in early April, watching the first day of Middlesex v Derbyshire, for which I had prepared by donning thermals from neck to ankle (a wise precaution, although the wintry sun did peep through the clouds once in a while). 'Just doing this makes us old buffers by definition,' he pronounced. But Adrian is as bald as a coot, he has three grandchildren, and his wattle is so pronounced he could probably smuggle drugs in it. We had to agree to disagree, as icicles started to form at the end of our noses.

A note on the title. 'Still a bit of snap in the celery' is a phrase Richard Ingrams invented to promote his magazine the *Oldie*, and Richard my publisher decided to steal it, there being no book with that title (until now). Its purpose is to suggest that while we might be getting on a bit, we are still fully functional (fill in obvious joke here). It has the benefit of being positive, because in the main my attitude towards the early sixties, where I now reside, is and remains positive, even though my fear of the future seems to grow daily. I liked 'Young/Old' but it was decided it was a bit 'Ronseal': it does what it says on the tin. This is not considered a good thing in publishing today, for reasons I don't wholly understand, but I can live with it. You do live with things at sixty-two. What does any of it matter in the long run?

The comedy of it all gets me. If you try to cut your toe-nails with anything less than a blowtorch, you are compelled to laugh, because the only alternative is stabbing someone with those now useless scissors. I have realised, in writing this book, that I am living through one of the most purely humorous phases of life, which may be why I laugh out loud if I happen to catch sight of my naked body in a mirror. (Our flat is full of mirrors, possibly as punishment for some long-forgotten crime.) Certainly my children, now in their early twenties, see me as a figure of fun, not to be taken entirely seriously until they run out of money and need to ask me for some.

But, like the Oldest Swinger in Town, I hang on slightly desperately to whatever of my youth remains to me, so I have decided to ignore Adrian, and I reject utterly his opinion that we are now just old. You may be, sunshine, but I am not. I find myself encouraged in this endeavour by the words of another friend of mine, who first read *A Shed of One's Own* in his late thirties. He thought it was hilarious. Then he read it again when he was forty-nine and thought it the most ter-rifying book he had ever read. I like that reaction. I would send him a copy of this book, if only I could remember which friend of mine this was, but as I said, I am now sixty-two, so obviously that would be too much to ask. If it was you, please let me know, and if it wasn't you, please don't pretend it was. So let's press on now, with an update on that most worrying of our various problems, the Body. Do you still have one? Is it complete and functioning within normal parameters, as they say on *Star Trek*? I very much hope so . . .

1

Body

When you are a child, you look down at your body and think, wow, that's rather neat. Five toes on each foot: who thought of that? You are small and compact and quite unlike those huge hairy adults who stop you eating Smarties at all times of day or night. One day, long in the future, you might grow into one of them, but as a child you never think about this. You are too busy running around and having energy. You cannot imagine a time in which you will not spend all your time running around and having energy. Lucky old you.

When you are an adolescent, you probably look down at your body with disgust. It's too fat, too thin, too misshapen, too hairy, not hairy enough, and you still have just the five toes, just like everyone else. You have an overwhelming desire to tattoo one of your toes, just to look different. You may well be astonishingly beautiful to all other age groups, but not to your own, and especially not to yourself. Is that the first inkling of a zit on your forehead? The world has come to an end.

When you are a young adult, you have a vital decision to

make: am I going to bother with my body or not? Are you going to look better and more handsome than you ought to, or can you not be bothered? Will you lose weight, or bulk up, or wear decent clothes, or develop a personality that will win friends and influence people? Or will you slob around in old sweatshirts, eat pizza every day for breakfast, maybe grow a disastrous beard that will put off everyone other than the insect life that will soon infest it? Or maybe you don't feel that this is your decision to make, that everything has been decided for you by your genes, your parenting, your environment and all the wrong decisions you have already made? Tough times, your twenties and early thirties. Some of us even start going bald, which is just testosterone laughing in your face.

In middle age, which seems to go on for ever, we get the first presentiments that the body does not come with an instruction manual. (Or, in the modern way, the manual is somewhere online, and you might get round to downloading it but you will never get round to reading it.) Bodies start doing strange things we weren't expecting. Noses and ears start sprouting hair where there was none before. Where once we could get away with only shaving every few days, some of us now have to shave almost hourly. You have lost the gloss of youth, to be replaced by the dull emulsion of middle age. Was that it? you ask your body. Yes, says your body, and you've blown it.

So once you reach sixty, you really have been through it. Your body is no longer the high-performance twin-camshaft speedster of your youth. It's now a sputtering Ford Escort with chronic rust. It's different for everyone, of course. Some of us have serious health problems, and one or two of us won't recover from them. But most of us are knocking along all right, negotiating the gradual transfer from the middle lane of life to the slow lane, behind all the lorries and the cars towing caravans. There's only one consolation in all this: when you look in the mirror first thing in the morning and see a half-mad seventy-five-year-old looking out at you, at least you know you probably have fifteen years before you look like that all day.

Ears

Just as women above a certain age cannot hide their scraggy necks or liver spots on their hands, because life is cruel like that, so men who have had all the plastic surgery in the world can do nothing about their ears. They just keep growing. If you had small ears to start, then by late middle age you will have normal-size ears, all the better for listening to things. If you had medium to large ears, the sky's the limit – literally, if you're in a high wind and you suddenly become airborne. Dumbo was not, as we had always previously assumed, a young elephant, but an old man with enormous ears. As we approach sixty, all the blood that previously ran to our sexual organs now goes to our ears. This is why they go an unpleasant shade of purple whenever you see an attractive woman.

My benchmark for enormous ears was always the film director David Lean, the sight of whose aural appendages now elicits a small gasp of shock from anyone who has never seen them before. It's like going into Tesco and seeing a woman with enormous silicone-enhanced breasts, when you had just dropped in to pick up some avocados. But at least she chose to have these things clamped on her chest. Lean could do nothing about his ears. There's no such thing as ear surgery. No one flies to Thailand to have their lobes reduced. In recent years Elton John's ears have expanded promisingly, although I feel they would look more in proportion if he didn't always have that cat asleep on his head. Quickly typing 'famous men with huge ears' into Google gleans a list that includes Will Smith, Russell Tovey, Daniel Craig, Gary Lineker and HM the King. It is of course a vicious irony that as your ears grow ever larger, their ability to perform their primary function declines ever more swiftly. Several of my contemporaries are now assuredly hard of hearing, and a few wear hearing aids, although you would barely know it, as these aids get smaller and less noticeable (if not actually more effective) with each passing year. My own hearing is OK, but my problem is tinnitus, which is loud and constant and takes out certain upper sound registers as if with a meat cleaver. This is what we learn with the body: that if it's not one thing, it's another. Tinnitus, of course, is completely incurable: you just have to get used to it. My doctor, who bought his bedside manner on the cheap, just sighed with inexpressible boredom when I told him of it. Couldn't I get ill slightly more interestingly? The doctor was about thirty-two. He has since died, although probably not from tinnitus.

We have left the best till last. ('Deferment of Gratification' could be my middle name.) Ear hair. I touched on this awkward subject in *Shed*, when I had at most two or three hairs growing from each ear, and plucking them out regularly (and painfully). Now there's a small copse in each lughole. In this house they are referred to as 'Daddy's ear shrubbery'. Why do they like it in there so much? Were these hairs always there, under the skin, from babyhood, waiting patiently for late middle age to strike? Occasionally you see a very old man with the usual huge ears and, inside them, a thicket so dense you would need a team of tiny gardeners wielding minuscule scythes to keep it under control. I used to see such men and think, Poor guy. Now I see them and think, My future.

Feet

No one is ever going to pretend that feet are things of beauty, except on tiny babies, obviously. But by adolescence they have already mutated into smelly, misshapen items often covered with unsightly hair and concealing all manner of fungal infections in their warmer, moister regions. Can it get any worse? By golly it can.

The feet of a sixty-year-old make you want to cry. As well as the toenails, which grow at the speed of sound and are so thick they are essentially indistinguishable from horn, the soles of your feet are now so well insulated with leathery layers of dead skin you could probably stick a drawing pin in them and not feel it. (Which isn't such a bad thing if you are prone to leaving drawing pins lying around.) The weird thing is that only some soles of some feet are affected. My right foot is as leathery as an old saddlebag, and I have to buff it with a pumice stone after every bath. My left foot isn't leathery at all. Why is that? Do I favour my right side, lean on my right foot more than my left? It doesn't feel as though I do, but then the sixty-year-old body is constantly telling you things you didn't know, and probably didn't want to know.

More mysterious still are the deep crevasses in the leathery sole, which obviously started off as ordinary creases in the skin but have since developed into mighty canyons, down which you could probably go on a decent adventure holiday if you felt so inclined. Not that they hurt or anything, but what I find weird is that the skin at the bottom of these megacreases is just as hard as the skin at the top. Which suggests that the dead skin goes a long way down, that your foot is even more leathery that you ever realised. Yes, I know, I should just put on some socks and forget about all this.

Skin

We all know that skin gets looser, loses its elasticity, as we get older, but this much? I seem to have so much more skin than I used to, more than I ever thought it possible to have, although not as much as some people, thank heavens. Our better-fed friends who lose lots of weight are very rarely told that they will retain all the skin that previously contained their excess poundage, and nor are they advised what they should do with it, where they should put it all. You can have plastic surgery to have it removed, but what happens if you put some of the weight back on? Will the remaining skin be able to do the job previously achieved by half as much skin again? I have no idea, but the phrase 'burst like a sausage' has just sprung into my mind.

I have always been quite a slim person, although like nearly everyone I am not quite as slim as I used to be. (We'll be addressing this subject more directly later.) But the skin is definitely showing its age. On my face it's now appreciably redder than before, which I attribute to sun damage, more than forty years of shaving and booze. My partner Polly has told me that I can no longer wear dark red shirts (a long-time favourite of mine) because 'they clash with your face'. Elsewhere it seems to be bearing up better, although there's no escaping the scraggy neck, the now prominent jowls, the patches of rough skin distributed randomly around the body, the slightly more pockmarked nose I seem to be getting, and the monumental eyebags, which recall for me the 1970s BBC newscaster Peter Woods, whose eyebags suggested that he was suffering some secret and profound sorrow, when he was really only thinking about what to have for dinner. If you have a long, lugubrious face, as Woods did, the eyebags only make you look more miserable. In fact, I suspect that age only accentuates what we perceive to be our worst features, and minimises or entirely wipes out what in youth were our natural physical advantages. You can try to fight this process of decay, with exercise: swimming, hefting weights around, jogging, the full monty of madness. Or you can eat the full monty of breakfast and stop worrying about any of it.

Hair

By the age of sixty you're lucky to have any hair left at all, and what there is has probably gone grey, or even white. For some reason it is perfectly acceptable for women to dye their hair all sorts of unusual colours, although I always feel slightly aggrieved when a young woman dyes her hair grey, in a wild display of careless youth, little knowing that the average age for Britons to start going grey for real is just thirty-four. (The hair gods are not mocked.) But when a man dyes his hair any colour at all, it looks ridiculous. Paul McCartney has had more hits than anyone and has more money that the King, but the distressing shade of bright purple he used for so many years on his hair made him a figure of fun, the Ted Rogers *de nos jours*. There's something about hair dye that accentuates the ageing, saggy face beneath, but only on men. If they also dye their beard, they just look like old mini-cab drivers, marinated in failure and disappointment.

That this is unfair is apparent, but at sixty you should have stopped saying life is unfair at least half a century before. The truth is that women are better at looking after themselves, because they have had a lifetime of being judged almost solely on appearances. So when they reach the nursery slopes of old age, they know what they are doing in a way that most straight men simply don't. (The gay men of my acquaintance tend to be better preserved.) A year or two ago I went to a college reunion of my contemporaries: my year, the year above and the year below. The women had all taken good care of themselves, and one or two were actually more attractive than they had been at twenty. (Genuinely so: it was a pleasant surprise.) Whereas the men, with a handful of exceptions, looked terrible. Huge bellies, disastrous combovers, great white beards, skin like overcooked gammon and, in one or two cases, an air of palpable defeat. One of them I had last seen when we graduated, when he was a rather chipper fellow with a decent line in dirty jokes and a Zapata-like black moustache. Now he was unimaginably small and frail with a huge white beard which looked as though it was growing him rather than the other way round. We had a brief chat, at the end of which he passed out, collapsed to the floor and had to be carried from the hall. I think he may have been quite seriously ill, although we didn't talk about it, because men never discuss such things, especially after not seeing each other for forty years. But what did stick in the mind is that he was at most eighteen months older than me.

This will sound like boasting – and even if it is, I don't much care – but I am one of the better-preserved specimens of my generation, with (very nearly) a full head of hair of which only the temples have gone grey. But I have always looked years younger than my age, and when I was twenty-five, looking fifteen was by no means an advantage. (The last time I was asked for ID when trying to buy alcohol, I was thirty-seven.) Although I aged rather disconcertingly during the Covid menace, and now really struggle to get out of the bath without hydraulic equipment, I feel this is payback time.

After I wrote *A Shed of One's Own*, I went to speak at a number of literary festivals about the horrors of being middle aged. At every literary festival I have ever been to, there is at least one furious man of late middle age or older, often sitting in the front row, with steam coming out of his ears. Whoever you are, whatever you have to offer, he hates your guts. (At the Hay Festival, there were three of the bastards, an all-comers' record.) So there I am, up on the stage, having talked the talk, and taking questions afterwards, as you do. Furious man puts his hand up.

'You dye your hair, don't you?'

No, I don't as it happens. This is entirely natural.

'You dye your hair, don't you?'

Not since the last time I looked, I don't.

'You dye your hair, don't you.' Note that this has ceased to be a question and become just a statement of 'fact'.

I take the next question, from a smiling lady in a nice hat.

More hair than before

We should never underestimate the sheer and lifelong trauma of losing your hair, because otherwise why would so many men invest in wigs and hair transplants? The alternative is to wear a silly little hat like the Edge of U2, who already has the burden of having renamed himself 'the Edge' sometime in his early twenties, an error he has almost certainly come to regret bitterly. There's a part of me that desperately wants him to take off the hat and say, Actually, my name's Dave and I'm as bald as your friend Adrian. And there's a rather bigger part of me that knows that this will never happen.

Wigs are a testament to man's vanity – which is fine, as we are allowed to be vain – but also to man's ineluctable foolishness. Every man wearing a wig walks down the street thinking, with great pleasure, I have a full head of hair. Everyone who passes him thinks, That man is wearing a catastrophic wig. Only a very few rugs manage to pull off the impossible, which is to be so like real hair it never even occurs to you to try to pull it off.* William Shatner's wig, which in many ways blighted my childhood, I have written about more times than is entirely healthy, but the one that really surprised me was Christopher Lee's, which I never guessed was a syrup for a moment, possibly because he had been wearing one in exactly the same swept-back style for more than fifty years. Would he have looked even more terrifying if he had taken it off?

---

* I feel certain that the desire to pull off another man's wig is one of those human universals, like the need to jump into a pile of autumn leaves on the pavement, or when you are waving around a pretend lightsabre, the need to go 'Zhummm! Zhummm!' under your breath.

I have more sympathy with people who get hair transplants, because although, like donning a rug, it's almost always a mistake, it's not one you can easily correct. Once installed, it's there for good. And while wigs are inexpensive, hair transplants cost upwards of £10,000, which is probably about a pound a hair. It's also supposed to be quite painful, when you are having it done. I can't imagine the level of psychological pain (horror at being bald) you must have to endure to go through the physical pain and the financial pain of having one put in, only to feel the pain of disappointment when it sits on your head like a stuffed ferret. If men actually talked about such stuff, their friends would always advise them against. But obviously men do not. When a friend of mine turned up to a get-together with a new hair transplant (to be fair, a very expensive and not bad-looking one), we all noticed, and no one said a word. There was an *omertà* of embarrassment. No one brought it up for a month or two. But I think the shock was not that he had done it at all, but that we had all thought of our friend as a supremely confident and assured character, and his hair transplant demonstrated that he was far more vulnerable than he had appeared. In that respect a hair transplant can say more about its owner than mere words ever can. Most of us had only known him thirty-five years or so.

Teeth

A few years ago, when I was in my late forties, I went to a couple's joint sixtieth birthday party, as you do. The party was full of people who were the same age then as I and my friends are now, and the one thing I noticed, because they all leant close to talk to you because the music was just that little bit too loud, was that many had the rankest breath imaginable. All of them were fighting a war against gum disease and tooth decay, and for several the war wasn't going too well. Casualty numbers were impossible to gauge, as everyone had a full set of teeth, one of two of which may still have been real. I remember nothing else about the party, which felt like a grim presentiment of my own future and that of my friends.

I think we are doing better than this, but only just. The smokers and heavy-duty coffee drinkers have breath you could probably walk on, but most of the rest of us seem to be able to pass among our fellow humans without making them want to throw up, which is a boon. We floss like maniacs, we clean our teeth hourly, we use those wonderful little TePe brushes to de-plaque the ever-widening gaps between our teeth, and every so often we go to the dentist for some unavoidable surgical intervention, the next step down the highway to gummy toothlessness and a gleaming set of plastic gnashers. In the past couple of years I have had a wisdom tooth pulled out, my first extraction, and another much-filled tooth was given a root canal, also my first. That tooth has had bits dropping off it ever since, and the dentist sent me off to a specialist to have it removed as well. And so it goes on, and in between visits to the hygienist my teeth have passed through the yellow stage, past ochre and are now verging on brown. Every time I catch sight of them in the mirror I blanch. They still work, just about, but there's now so much mercury in my mouth my days of passing through the airport metal detector without setting off all the alarms must surely be numbered.

All this, of course, costs unimaginable amounts of money. Did anyone tell us when we are young that most of the savings we were trying (and mainly failing) to accrue would be spent on dental bills? When you go to the bank to borrow more, they often ask you what you need it for. Pay off credit card bills, you say, or buy a run-down rustheap of a car to replace your current rustheap. No one mentions their troublesome top right molar.

The British, though, are believed to have legendarily bad teeth, mainly by Americans, who all had theirs done years ago. Even the most decrepit oldie in the US seems to have perfect, gleaming white teeth, whether or not they regularly appear on primetime TV. I think I'd prefer bad breath to that. One or two friends of mine have had their teeth whitened, and the effect is utterly discombobulating, as though you had taken your old rustheap of a car, replaced its radiator with a brand new one from a current model, and left the rest of the vehicle the same. When the cricketer, later commentator Shane Warne had his teeth whitened, he would appear on Sky Sports and grin threateningly, as though to say, these teeth cost me a fortune. Blinded by his gnashers, we, the viewers, stopped listening to what he was saying and just stared at his teeth. I often wondered whether the teeth contributed in some way to his ridiculously early death, aged fifty-two, just after a massage in a Thai hotel. The future's so bright you gotta wear shades.

Stomachs

Although a few of my friends retain their slim, lithe, youthful figures, having sold their souls to Beelzebub, most of us continue to pile on the pounds.* 'How did I get so fat?' asked a prosperous-looking friend of mine. By eating at least two huge meals a day, I didn't say, and never doing any exercise, other than walking to and from the fridge. Men who were quite large at fifty are now absolutely vast. You would have thought their bodies had reached their limits some time ago, but it turns out there's always room for one more curry, and there will be room for another one tomorrow. A friend of a friend is what is known as a trencherman. The three of us met in a pub for a drink at around seven o'clock, but it turned out the pub wasn't doing food. The trencherman looked panicked, then increasingly desperate. Where was he going to get his next enormous meal from? He started sweating, couldn't concentrate on our conversation. Then at about a quarter to eight he cracked, and fled to the Indian restaurant he had noticed round the corner. I realised then that greedy people are always on the lookout for nearby restaurants in case of emergency. The trencherman has been told by his doctor that if he doesn't stop eating and drinking too much right now, if not sooner, he will die. He told us this while holding a glass of red wine about the size of a swimming pool.

Back of the knee

This is said to be the only part of the body that doesn't have a proper name, other than 'back of the knee'. I think I may

---

* In July 2020 *Saga Magazine* polled 8,500 of its customers, few of whom will see fifty-five again. Of these, 76 per cent weigh more than they did in their twenties, and 46 per cent of men had gone up two or more clothes sizes. Forty per cent said their weight gain had begun in their fifties. The rest of them, presumably, were lying.

have found another. When fat men go bald, or bald men get fat (either will do), they develop a strange little horizontal fold at the back of their head, just above the hairline. It is very much not a thing of beauty, and is particularly noticeable on angry bald fat men whose pint has not been poured to their satisfaction. At such moments the fold can seem like a symbol of all their manifold disappointments, one of those things that was only going to happen to someone else, and not you. But here's a thing. I am neither fat nor bald, but I have exactly the same fold, invisible to all but me, feeling it with my fingers and translating that information to the mind's eye. There is no escape from any of this, and to think otherwise is only to fool yourself.

Face shape

This is one Polly noticed and passed on to me, like a small bar of plutonium during an unusually perilous game of pass the parcel. In our early sixties our faces begin to change shape. If you always had a round face, as I did, it gets longer; if you always had a long face, it gets even longer. At the same time your eyes recede, giving you a myopic look you may never have had before. Why? How does this work? Who does it possibly benefit? Are we supposed to end up barely recognisable to ourselves, let alone to other people?

Bladder and prostate

One thing we all know about getting older is that your bladder seems to function less effectively. You wake up in the middle of the night and need a pee. Then you start waking up a second time needing a pee, and after that you can't get back to sleep because you have started to worry about your prostate, which is the real villain in all this. An enlarged prostate gland is, not always but occasionally, a stepping stone to prostate cancer, which could mean a prostatectomy and all sorts of nastiness I really don't want to think about.

So far, I have been lucky: I rarely need to get up to do a pee before the very early morning. Nonetheless, I was in a pub the other day with a tiny loo and only one urinal, which was occupied by a young person. On and on he peed, splashing away unceasingly. I was standing nearby, gagging to go, and trying to guess how many milk bottles he would have filled with his urine tsunami. Two, maybe? Three? At home our only loo is in the bathroom and my son, aged twenty, likes to have incredibly long baths, to the point that it is worth checking from time to time that he is still alive. My bladder used to be such a patient organ, but now its needs must be addressed rather more swiftly. So I know from bitter experience that even if I have been desperate to go for a pee for ages, I will rarely fill more than half a milk bottle. The outside of the bottle, the dry bit, is also disconcertingly warm after I have peed into it. Has my pee always been warm? There's another thought I didn't need in my head.

So, on a friend's advice, I went to get my prostate checked out by a doctor wearing rubber gloves. Long and short of it: it's fine. A great sigh of relief. I remembered the playwright Simon Gray going for a thorough medical when he was in his seventies. Do you want the good news or the bad news first? said the doctor, who obviously fancied himself as a bit of a comedian. The good news, said Gray. You've got prostate cancer, said the doctor. That's the good news? said Gray.

Well, it's not going to kill you, said the doctor. The bad news is that there are so many other things wrong with you one of them will get you first.

Here's the good news. Nature has devised a simple way to keep your prostate in good condition: regular ejaculation. Milking the gonads, with or without the aid of the internet, or if you're really lucky, sex with a proper human being, is good for you. But that's enough on that subject.

2

Aches and Pains

As well as all the areas of specific physical decline, there is also a more general, less easily identifiable slippage towards senescence that shows itself in all sorts of unexpected ways. Six or seven years ago my leg muscles were sufficiently strong that I could get out of the bath without using my hands at all. I was quite proud of this. Somewhere along the line this became difficult, and then impossible. Now, as previously alluded to, when I get out of the bath, it's with a mighty physical effort and lots of undignified grunting. Can I put this down to something in particular? No, it's just getting older.

Supposing something falls on the floor. In the old days you would go and pick it up. Now, you first look around to see if there's anybody else who could pick it up. You might call someone in from another room on a spurious pretext. Then, just as they are leaving, you ask them if they could pick it up. If no one is available, you might start asking yourself awkward questions. Is there an urgent need to pick this thing up right now? Can it wait a bit? Does it look quite comfortable on the floor, as though it was always meant to be there?

It doesn't really matter how you look. It's how you move that makes you seem young or old. Often it's whether you move at all. Years spent on a chair staring at a screen, then coming home and sitting in an armchair staring at a screen, can take a brutal toll. When you want to move after a long time in the same place, you find that you can't: your body has seized up. If there was a human equivalent of WD-40, life would be unimaginably enhanced. If you had a mechanic standing by to oil your joints every few hours, you could probably run a marathon.*

Aches and pains are natural and, normally, mean nothing. But we are all on the lookout for the apparently harmless symptom that could lead on to something slightly less harmless and, to cut a rather horrible long story short, agonising death. Aches and pains make hypochondriacs of us all, and there's a good reason for this, which is that after you have hit sixty, people will start dying on you. The first symptom was trivial enough. They turned bright blue, or started speaking Estonian. But one thing has a tendency to lead to another, and soon you are getting your funeral suit dry-cleaned again.

I knew very few people who died in their forties and fifties, and those who did seemed very unlucky. But I have known quite a lot of people who died in their sixties, and when you now tell someone younger that that seems very young to die, they look at you as though you are mad. Mortality starts picking us off like characters in a disaster movie. (Maybe, in this sense, we actually are all characters in a disaster movie.)

---

* Or maybe not. Appearing on *The Chase: Celebrity Special*, Sir Geoff Hurst was asked by host Bradley Walsh whether he missed playing football. 'Of course not,' said Sir Geoff. 'I'm a man in my seventies. I can't do that running around any more.'

But here's a thing. I think it's fair to say that sixty is the first landmark age at which you could easily live another thirty-five, even forty years ... or you could keel over next week. There's no way of knowing. Would you wish to know if you could? Obviously not. The glorious uncertainty of life is one of the things that makes it worth living. But it does get you thinking. A novelist friend of mine, roughly the same age as me, has been writing books for nearly thirty years, and she says that only now does she feel she is getting the hang of it. And suddenly, as from nowhere, mortality begins to loom. She wonders, quite seriously, how many books will she be able to produce in the time she has left. Half a dozen? Three? One? None at all?

Thus do aches and pains tower over us, influence our conscious thoughts and beg to be interpreted, usually incorrectly. Is that just a stomach ache or the first inkling of stomach cancer? It's a stomach ache, you fool. My mother, whenever something starts to hurt, goes straight to her medical encyclopaedia, and once she has spent half an hour leafing through it, she has convinced herself that she has everything, from a bad cold to hepatitis C via shingles and legionnaires' disease. Once she persuaded herself that she had both Hodgkin's lymphoma and non-Hodgkin's lymphoma, which isn't bad for a day's work. She is ninety-one and in almost perfect health. Whenever she goes to the doctor, the doctor of the day asks her what medication she is on. None, says my mother. Why not? asks the doctor. Don't need any, says my mother. The doctor is inevitably dumbfounded, and says that he (or she) has never heard of anyone aged ninety-one who wasn't on some form of medication. You have now, says my mother, a steely glint in her eye.

Not counting my mother, who is interested in symptoms as she is in her family tree, as a harmless leisure activity, I have known four cast-iron, 24-carat, ocean-going hypochondriacs, each of whom could have represented their country in the Hypochondria Olympics. All four of them are and always have been in perfect health. Two are in their eighties, two in their fifties. They talk about their health constantly, and all four despise doctors because they can never find anything wrong with them. The simple question 'How are you?' elicits not the required 'Fine, thanks,' but a fifteen-minute monologue, actually answering the bloody question. I have a theory that it is complaining about their health that keeps them so fit, and there may be some truth in it, for oncologists often remark that it is the most ornery, cantankerous and plain contrarian of their patients who outlive their prognosis, often by years. While the good boys and girls, the passive ones who do what they are told, die relatively swiftly. (As someone inclined not to make a fuss if at all possible, this chills me to the marrow.)

I can see why you might become a hypochondriac, though, because you only need to have suffered one serious health problem in your life to know that health trumps everything. The ill know what the healthy do not, which is that their problems, however pressing, fade almost to nothing because they still have their health. I have a friend who has suffered chronic ill health for the past eighteen months. There's nothing that annoys him more than his healthy but self-centred friends moaning on about their terrible divorces, awful children and lack of money as he sits in his armchair trying desperately to breathe.

So I write this chapter knowing, or rather hoping, that

there's nothing seriously wrong with me, and feeling thankful for that. But there remain, as always now, these little aches and pains. I feel a bit like an old pair of shoes you've just had repaired, and then the following day the shoelace breaks. Here are my aches and pains of the moment, in no particular order:

Dodgy elbow. This appears to be a repetitive strain injury from lifting heavy books to perch my laptop on when doing an online quiz. I don't think it's tennis elbow, which I have obviously researched thoroughly (i.e. read a few things on the internet about). The pain is in the forearm, just south of the actual elbow, and will probably go away if I just rest it. At lunch in a pub the other day I asked a friend about his tennis elbow. He told me at considerable length, barely pausing for breath.

Knees made of biscuit. I used to run upstairs all the time and everywhere, but now my knees hurt too much and a lot of the time I have to trudge upstairs like everyone else. This is depressing as I now realise I was someone who enjoyed running upstairs, that it gave me pleasure in itself, and that I also enjoyed being the sort of person who runs upstairs. Because I have always been a sprinter rather than a long-distance runner, running upstairs used less energy than walking up them, because it was a burst of energy, easily recovered from. From time to time I still run upstairs, even though I know that my knees will hurt like buggery for some time afterwards, because I am unwilling to completely let go of who I once was. This is a common theme in ageing.

Watery eyes. This is very recent, and makes me look as though I have just been weeping copiously, which of course I haven't, being the strong and silent type. My mother, who looked it up in her medical encyclopaedia, diagnosed vitamin

A deficiency, and bought me some chewy sweets to consume, two a day with meals. No effect at all. My theory is that it's a secondary symptom of the hay fever that has been creeping up on me over the past few years. As so often, merely typing the word 'hay fever' just then has made want to sneeze.

Wheat intolerance. I love saying the words 'wheat intolerance' to right-wing hufnpufs and watching the steam come out of their ears. But it definitely exists. Fifteen years ago I had a number of small but irritating ailments: bloating, indigestion, insomnia, a tendency to fall asleep at inconvenient moments. I was diagnosed with gluten intolerance – a classic case, I was told – and advised that those three Weetabix I was eating every morning for breakfast were not doing my guts any good at all. Cut out bread, wheaty cereals and that second packet of biscuits and you'll soon feel the difference. And I did. Seventy-two hours without gluten and the indigestion and the bloating ceased, and I felt better than I had for years.

Not so long ago I was told by a kinesiologist that it wasn't gluten my digestive system couldn't tolerate, it was just wheat. Actually, I had spotted this myself, as I could still drink lager (made with barley) by the bucketload. But as long as I moderate my wheat intake, I am fine. The problem is pizzas, which I adore. A doughy or deep pan pizza will give me a brutal wheat hangover, which usually means passing out for two hours and waking up feeling that you have eaten a breezeblock. But a thin crust pizza has a less savage effect, and sourdough pizzas, amazingly, have little or no effect at all. Of course one can become obsessed, and I have friends with dodgy digestion who meet and talk about their food intolerances for hours, exchanging war stories like old soldiers remembering long forgotten campaigns of the past.

Morning arthritis. This is a new one. I know none of us look our best in the morning, and after the age of forty-five it's advisable not to look in the mirror at all until midday. Not being able to see yourself until you put your glasses on is one of the best arguments for glasses yet devised.

But recently I have also noticed that, first thing, my joints ache like billy-o and my feet don't really feel like feet, but like newly hatched centres of pain. So going downstairs to the loo, which is something I can normally do without thinking, becomes more perilous. How many more stairs to go? I'm not sure, so I have to stop and go down each step more carefully. Falling downstairs and crashing your head against the wall before you have even had a cup of tea would not be a good look.

Tinnitus. As previously mentioned, I have this in both ears and it's the high-pitched version, which is apparently more bearable than the low-pitched grumbly variety. William Shatner had it after an explosion went wrong in the original *Star Trek* series, and he said it nearly drove him mad, to the extent that he actually agreed to appear in *T. J. Hooker*.

Tremor. A few years ago, I noticed my handwriting beginning to deteriorate. This was unexpected, and a bit disappointing, as my handwriting had always been a source of pride to me: it was clear and distinctive, even beautiful, and the main reason I was always given the pen at pub quizzes. How many writers' careers start as an offshoot of their pleasure in their handwriting? But it was increasingly scratchy and effortful, the formation of letters requiring greater concentration and often not actually leading to the correct ones being formed. Ns, Ms and Ws were particularly challenging.

At the same time, I noticed that as I carried the morning

cup of tea upstairs, the spoon in the cup was often jangling against the side. Was my hand shaking? Either that or my hand was still and the rest of my body was shaking. I went to the doctor. She looked concerned and referred me to a neurologist at the hospital down the road.

A mere five months later my appointment came up and I trooped off to Dr X, who like all the best doctors was extremely hirsute, which seems to grant them an authority less furry doctors can only dream about. Or maybe, as he does his various tests on you, the huge tufts of hair poking out from his collar and the ends of his sleeves operate as a useful distraction. But he was nothing if not thorough. He said there are two types of tremor, a tremor at rest and a tremor in action. A tremor at rest, when you're just sitting there not doing anything, often turns out to be Parkinson's. Fortunately, he said, you have a tremor in action. It's what we call an essential tremor, which means that it is what it is and nothing else. There are no nasty consequences down the road, although it will probably get worse over time. We can treat it with beta blockers if you wish. I shook my head. Beta blockers, for someone who relies for his living on what is going on inside his head, are a bit like cutting off your leg to remove a splinter. How long have I had it? Oh, quite a while, said Dr Werewolf. These things creep up on you. Maybe four or five years.

Which got me thinking. I have played cricket, and run a shambolic team, since I was nineteen, but for the past four or five years the very few things I could do on a cricket field had deserted me. I could always take a catch, but now I was dropping them. I could always stay at the crease when batting, hold an end up, although I very rarely scored any runs. Now

I was getting out quickly for 0 every time. This wasn't just getting on a bit, this was the tremor. Which *is* a manifestation of getting on a bit, of course. Not being able to do what you used to do with a laugh and a skip is what getting older is all about. My body hasn't yet committed a major felony, but the misdemeanours are beginning to mount up.

3

Masculinity

A few years ago my old economics teacher celebrated his sixtieth birthday, and invited some of his favourite pupils to a posh dinner in the private room of a members' club. Although I only got a D in my A level, I somehow qualified, as did my old friend C, who was the only other person in the room I had seen for more than a quarter of a century. Some of the others I recognised immediately. One looked exactly the same as he had at the age of eighteen, except a little more worn around the edges, and his fine mop of curly black hair had been replaced by a bald head, surrounded by a rather smaller mop of curly black hair. But there were others I didn't recognise at all. I have always had a good memory for faces, and have often seen schoolboys of my era wandering around the parks of north London, slightly fatter, slightly older, surrounded by their burgeoning families. So who were these people? One of them recognised me but his face wasn't familiar. He just looked like any other slightly eroded man in a suit in his mid-forties. Do you remember me? he asked, and I had to admit I did not. Fortunately there was a photo of us all in school uniform, from twenty-five years before. Eroded man in a suit pointed out a rather beautiful boy with the shoulder-length hair we all sported in 1977, and sighed audibly. He knew, and I knew he knew, that he now bore literally no resemblance whatsoever to the jailbaity little princess he had once been. (It was an all-boys school.) I would have thought that would have been a matter of some relief – he must have been fighting them off with sticks – but clearly not. Better to look like that then, however perilous it might have been, than to look like this now.

How can we ever know what we are going to look like later in life? I don't think this is a thought that ever crosses our minds – not when we are young, anyway. Life is all about the present, and if we think of the future at all, it's in mainly economic and demographic terms: will we ever be able to afford to buy a house, will we have a family, will we thrive in our jobs, and so on. Not: will we go ridiculously bald like the man with the curly black hair, or will our faces fall apart. You don't really think about any of this until it's too late.

I have lived in the same area – I am going to be honest here: in the same flat – since 1988, so I have seen quite a few people get older, people I generally know only by sight. One fellow, roughly a contemporary I would say, was big in every way: large-boned, strong-featured, big hands, muscles, lairy expression on his face. He was, in other words, a scary bastard, the sort of person a wuss like me instinctively avoids, for reasons of personal preservation. All the violent acts Tom the cat suffers in the *Tom and Jerry* cartoons, especially those perpetrated by the perpetually enraged dog Spike, I could imagine this bloke doing to me if I so much as asked him the time.

But like everyone, the scary bastard has aged. The muscles turned to fat, the hair went white, and the lairy expressions softened. Obviously he has mellowed, and I am less of a wuss than I used to be, but the decisive factor is that, somewhere along the line, his face changed. Instead of looking dangerously psychopathic, he now looks slightly silly. I see him in the pub sometimes and my first thought is that he now resembles an enormous glove puppet. You could no more be frightened of him than of one of the Teletubbies.

What is a silly face? As so often in life, pop stars can help us here. The lead singer of Aerosmith, Steven Tyler, father of Liv, was unusually good looking as a young man, but now, with his smallish features, enormous lips, long hair and characteristic look of drug-fuelled bemusement, he has come to look very silly indeed. An internet meme of a few years ago had a photo of Ronnie Wood and Paul Weller and was captioned thus: 'My Nan and her friend Pauline have been missing since Monday. Both are vulnerable. Please help.'* There's a whole website dedicated to ageing male pop stars who now look like ciggy-raddled grandmas straight from the bingo. We shouldn't laugh but we do, really rather loudly.

A silly face is one that has lost its shape, lost its underlying threat, and has softened to the point of banality. Look at Ozzy Osbourne, who was actually quite handsome as a youth, and slightly more terrifying (because so unpredictable) in his thirties and forties. Now, slack of lip and rheumy of eye, his face has gone very silly indeed.

---

* Via @SearchDogKizzy on Twitter: https://twitter.com/SearchDogKizzy/status/818927730062491648

'Underlying threat' is important here. I mentioned that I went to an all-boys school, where the main currency of fear was physical strength. If you were tall and broad and had psychotic tendencies, they usually made you head of school. I was small and weedy and learned very quickly to keep my head down. Although I was bright, it did not pay to broadcast your intelligence unless you had the muscles to back it up. The teachers seemed to like the yobs more than they liked the clever boys: it didn't occur to me at the time that some of them were probably scared of the yobs, many of whom were bigger than them. The headmaster blatantly kowtowed to the yobs, but he was a weak man whose grand ambitions (headmastership of Rugby) were obliterated by his manifest inadequacies. As a result of all this, for many years I genuinely believed that physical strength was the single most important attribute a man could have. It was an unexpected delight of my adult years to discover that this wasn't the case.

I have often wondered what happened to the yobs at my school. Many of them were as thick as a turd sandwich, and so may have ended up as bouncers, or personal trainers, or cat food, none of which require decent A levels. One of them, cleverer than the rest, who either cheated in his A levels or put around the rumour that he had successfully cheated in his A levels to show everyone how hard he was, became a news reporter for a tabloid, which seems about right. But the rest of them have stories I find I would quite like to know. Have they become flabby and old like everyone else? Have they acquired silly faces? Do they still want to hit me into the middle of next week?

There was actually very little violence at my school, but the possibility of violence was ever present. The phrase 'toxic masculinity' is a relatively new one, but the phenomenon is as old as humanity. An all-boys school is a giant Petri dish for toxic masculinity. Its winners become life's bullies, because nothing has shown them that bullying people doesn't work. Their reliance on physical strength is replaced by an arrogance and a straightforward lack of interest in other people that will carry them through life like a stretch limo, often to positions of great power and influence.

And yet old age is waiting in the shadows for the toxics, as it is for the rest of us. Even the most arrogant and pompous of men will wither and decline sooner or later, and one of the best reasons for staying alive, I would say, is to be on hand to witness this. All we can really ask of life is to survive our enemies. I have already outlived one or two, and it warms the cockles of my heart to know that their hearts' cockles will never again be warmed by anything.

Back to that catastrophic modern invention, the mirror. One of the fundamental differences between men and women is that when women look in the mirror, they only see their flaws, even when they don't have any. Whereas men look in the mirror and think, Yeah, that'll do, even when it obviously won't. The over-confidence of hideous-looking men is an extraordinary thing, almost a form of mental illness in itself.

But as I said earlier, when a young/oldie gets up in the morning and looks in the mirror, he sees a hideous vision of himself in fifteen years' time, the shock of which can actually age a man visibly. As caffeine performs its wondrous work, our faces settle down and by mid-morning we look like human beings again. We look in the mirror if not with pride, certainly with relief.

Or here's another way of looking it at – your reflection, that is. As you see yourself in the mirror, you realise that that is the best you are ever going to look again. Ageing only goes in one direction. In a year's time, you will look worse. It's distinctly possible that tomorrow afternoon you will look worse. Today, now, is as good as it will ever be.

This is by no means a cheering thought. To be honest I'm surprised that more sexagenarians don't go straight to Dignitas. In fact, a friend of mine has told me, in confidence, that he is planning to do just that. Just sixty, he says he plans to top himself before he is seventy-five. He feels it would be undignified to go on any further. That sounds frivolous, and it did sound slightly frivolous when he told me, but I can assure you he is deadly serious. The idea of living to an advanced old age hooked up to various beeping machines and taking fifty-three tablets every morning appeals to him not at all. What makes it worse is that at the time both his parents were still alive and pushing ninety. (His father has since died, in his early nineties.) Their quality of life wasn't up to much and he felt they were just getting in the way. He doesn't intend to make the same mistake.

I am more cheerful and presume, almost certainly erroneously, that I shall live to a hundred in good health and high spirits, loved by everyone. But then you see a photograph of yourself five years ago and your first thought is, How young I was! It's hard to stay upbeat with all this evidence mounting up. My suggestion is: never look in the bloody mirror, even to shave.

George Orwell once made the famous assertion that at the age of forty, every man has the face he deserves. That was probably fair enough in an era of poor diet and even worse dentistry. Martin Amis raised the threshold to fifty, and I am now formally putting it up to sixty. Your face reflects what it has been through, and in sixty years it has been through a lot. If you spent most of those years smiling and laughing, you will have laughter lines. If you have spent those years being miserable, you will have deep frown lines that speak of your great suffering. Or, through an accident of biology, you may be happy and just look as though you're miserable. For women, it's known as 'resting bitch face', a phrase so wonderful it now has its own Wikipedia page. I'm not sure what the male equivalent would be – resting bastard face, maybe? – but my friend R has it. He looks woebegone even when he is deliriously happy. 'Why the long face?' people ask him hilariously, which actually does make him quite miserable.

So there is luck, and there are genes, and there is the accumulation of life's little peccadilloes, all of them reflected in your face and seen, and judged, by everyone. There are also smoking, drink and drugs, each of which can ravage a physiognomy. We have all seen examples of 'smoker's face': indeed, I have often thought that the only way to persuade the young either never to smoke or to give up immediately is to show them some faces of older people who still puff away. Drinkers get bright red noses. There's a boozer who lives up the road from me whose bright red nose has spread into a bright red face. If he wore an orange shirt and green trousers, you would think he was a traffic light. Drugs have all sorts of deleterious effects. Heroin is a preservative, which is why some of its more enthusiastic consumers start to look embalmed. Cocaine gives people fatal heart attacks before the age of forty, or makes you look like Danniella Westbrook. And even worse than smoker's face and cocaine face is crystal meth face. The before and after shots are terrifying. You may be old before you had a chance to be young, and you may be dead before you had a chance to be old.

And yet you can be entirely blameless, you can have led a good and modest life, and still have a face like a squished tomato. There's a bloke on the next road along from me, who lives alone, rarely leaves his flat, watches his wall-mounted cinema-screen-sized telly from dawn to dusk, and has a face so strikingly unfortunate you realise you have no idea how old he is. If he is really unlucky he may be thirty-five. I doubt he is over sixty because there is little grey in his hair and his paunch has yet to come into full flower. And yet I saw him leave his flat the other day, lollop down the road like a member of an alien species and get into a brand-new white Mercedes convertible with the lid down. So what's that all about? I haven't a clue, but I am desperate to find out.*

Can we try to resist the ageing process? Is it even possible? One time-honoured method is to grow a beard. Beards confer an often entirely spurious authority on a face, especially if that face has gone silly underneath. Ship's captains often grow beards, because they make it so much easier to bark out orders at underlings. Imagine Captain Birdseye without a beard. Or rather, don't, because it is literally impossible to do so.

Old age isn't kind to testosterone levels in the male body,

---

* Since I first wrote this his girlfriend/wife has moved in. She is small and Asian, and one of my neighbours, who also makes up stories about people he doesn't know who live on the next road, has theorised that she is a Thai bride, almost certainly (he believes) purchased on the dark web. She walks half a dozen steps behind alien-species man like a servant, but then gets into the front seat of his Mercedes convertible. He still watches telly at all hours of the day and night, though.

and most of what's left seems dedicated to the industrial production of ear hair and pubic eyebrows. But one possible advantage of being older, if you feel so inclined, is the ability to grow a much fuller beard than you might have been capable of when younger. I have never been a hairy man, but my facial hair has come on apace in the past five years or so, and I could now grow a halfway respectable beard without looking like Shaggy out of *Scooby-Doo*. Not that I will, because after five or six days it begins to itch like the blazes. Also, I shall admit that the younger generation's recent predilection for enormous beards has put me off. I believe that the trend for young men to grow huge unruly beards, and thereby wipe out the few years in which most of them will be attractive to the female population, will eventually turn out to have been a demographic error of cosmic proportions. Birth rates are falling and young women are always complaining there are no single men available to give them babies, and obviously there are, but a lot of them are concealed behind ridiculous beards.

For a young/oldie less scrupulous than I, however, there are many good reasons for growing a beard. For one, shaving turns out to be the single most boring thing in the world, especially after forty years. For another, beards may conceal the terrible ravages of time, and not just silliness of face, either. Tom Jones grew a beard to hide the scars from a bit of plastic surgery under his chin. And finally, it's a straightforward signal of masculinity, easily grown at a point in your life when there may not be many other such signals available.

What type of beard should you grow? There are many different varieties to consider, and each says more about you than cash ever can. I have a friend who has grown that tiny little beardette under the lower lip, which allegedly boasts an expertise in providing cunnilingus. Unfortunately, young women take one look at him and run screaming, while his wife gives him a look that suggests that he had better not try anything on her either or he won't know what hit him. Here are a few alternatives.

Goatee. This neat mouth-and-chin growth is believed by many to indicate thoughtfulness, especially if worn with thick horn-rimmed glasses and an expression of world-weary ennui. The problem is that it's therefore most frequently grown by thickies who want to appear thoughtful when there's nothing even resembling a thought running through their head. Unless it's which of the *Fast and Furious* films they're going to watch when they get home.

Full Naval, or the Polar Explorer. This one suggests that you are simply far too preoccupied by more important matters to give something so trivial as facial hair any thought at all. Predominantly worn by outdoor types with loud voices, and regularly spotted on ice shelves, the bridges of ocean-going ships and George V. Disadvantages include the absolute impossibility of not playing with it for most of the day and the tendency to get food stuck in it at every meal. Your friends may think they can see insects crawling around in it, and they will be right.

Full W. G. Grace. One up from the Full Naval, when the beard becomes so huge it overwhelms the face. Useful for escaping war criminals and weedy web designers from east London who can't quite face getting a tattoo to show how hard they are. White-bearded oldies who grow the full W. G. Grace will almost certainly have to put up with being addressed as 'Santa' by laughing children in the street, before being offered well-paid jobs as Santa every December.

The Bee Gee. Is it really a beard or just stubble with attitude? What it does tell passers-by is that you think and care way too much about your beard, which is the antithesis of male behaviour since time immemorial, or at least ageing male behaviour. The Bee Gee only works if it looks accidental, which is incredibly hard to get right, as it clearly isn't accidental at all.*

The Statement Beard. These are a relatively recent development, and suggest to me that humanity's decline may be terminal. The Circle Beard runs in a thinnish line from the neck to the ears, before looping up and over the top of the owner's head, the rest of which has been shaven. As the *Guardian* put it, 'Imagine Saturn, but the planet is a human face and the rings are made of hair.' Or there's the Monkey-Tail Beard, where fully bearded men shave bits of their face so that the remaining hair forms a curl around their mouth. Or there's the Double Moustache, where people grow an exact duplicate of their moustache under their mouths.

It's a bit like wearing unusual or wacky glasses. Distinctive, for sure, but the question you have to ask yourself is: am I wearing the glasses, or are the glasses wearing me? Growing a statement beard, you become beard first, man second. People will look at you and think, Silly beard. Whatever statement you were trying to make, it probably wasn't that.

There is only one other way for the young/oldie to reassert his masculinity, but it's expensive and exhausting: have more

---

* Have you noticed how men in car ads always have Bee Gee beards? Maybe the ridiculous ad men who write and cast these things have unknowingly internalised the lyrics from 'Stayin' Alive': 'You can tell by the way I use my walk / I'm a woman's man, no time to talk'.

children. With your original partner, who is probably about the same age as you, this is of course impossible, so the ageing fools among us will junk her and start going out with some luscious young lovely whose ovaries are beginning to rumble. For as the desire for procreation does begin to loom, and as so many young men have enormous beards, their best bet may be some silly-faced, ageing imbecile who has more money than brain cells and is led by his penis as dogs are led by their noses.

Actually, I have two friends who became fathers in their fifties and their stories don't quite tally with this. One had been told many years before that that he had a low sperm count and would never be able to have children, so he and his girlfriend (twenty years younger) shagged away like rodents and one day, to their astonishment, she discovered she was pregnant. Their daughter is as loved as it is possible for a child to be.

The second never thought he was going to have kids as he was too much of a gadabout, in love with life's pleasures. Then at the age of nearly forty he met and fell in love with an actual woman, had two kids with her and discovered, to his delight, that this was what he had been put on earth to do. Eventually that relationship foundered, but my friend, after a period of savage decline, found his second wife, who was edging towards forty and keen to pop out a couple more while she had time. He is now the contented father of four.

And yet, and yet. Exceptionally happy though I know they both are, I have never seen two men age so quickly and so devastatingly as these did in the first few years of their children's lives. What had been manageable for the second one in his early forties (and for me at the same age) was very much not so in his early fifties. Both were hands-on dads, as you would expect them to be, and their hands were visibly shaking by the time their children had finished with them. Maybe that's a price worth paying, and they would insist it was. But for men after the age of fifty, having (more) children should probably carry a health warning. It's the fast track to old age, which is not somewhere you want to reach too quickly.

There's another type of man who has millions of children: the damaged man. The malignant narcissist. The psychopath. A recent blond-haired prime minister instantly comes to mind as a possible candidate. These men aren't particularly interested in the children they sire – some aren't remotely interested, other than as symbols of their own fertility and manliness – but they go on having them, because they can, and because they can afford to. They rarely look after their children in any practical sense, for they see their responsibility as paying for everything, and they derive most of their pleasure from complaining that they have to pay for everything. My father, now ninety, is one such man, who has between seven and nine children, depending on who you believe. The first daughter, older than me, is believed to have sprung from the loins of his first wife, who was by rumour a Turkish belly dancer (she probably isn't any more). This might be true, or it might just be a story: no one knows. I am the next child down, from his second wife, and there are six more after me, via various partners and wives. The putative ninth is a baby his 'housekeeper' gave birth to a few years ago. (She may even be his housekeeper as well as his 'housekeeper': I have no information on that.) My father is hugely rich, although sadly none of his cash will come to me as I have refused to have anything to do with him since 1975. I am hoping he lives until 2025, when we will celebrate a full half-century of no-speakers. (Separately, I hope.)

My father once told my mother that he only likes children until the age of five, because at that point they become too independently minded and are apt to have their own opinions. Merely this observation, you would have thought, would have had him banned from further parenthood by international law, but no, they keep popping out of various women's bodies, to be loved briefly and then rejected before they know what has hit them.

Does it seem fair that old men can still make babies when old women simply cannot? There's a picture of James Doohan, Scotty from *Star Trek*, gummy and semi-gaga, holding his newborn son or daughter at the age of eighty-three, and probably thinking it's a cat or a ferret. But it has recently been established that sperm declines in quality as we age, and old men's spermatozoa, hobbling with a stick rather than swimming vigorously up the birth canal, are often responsible for birth defects and all sorts of health problems down the line. The lesson is simple: keep it in your trousers, for your own sake and for everyone else's, if anyone else's concerns interest you at all.

4

Work

One of the main functions of masculinity is work. Primitive man went out, killed bison, picked berries, brought home a meal for his family to eat. Civilised man goes off on the 8.22 with his briefcase, but in his mind he is still killing bison, even though it's his wife who is going to Tesco that morning to pick up some shrink-wrapped bison steaks after pilates. Work, for many men, has become our *raison d'être*, our way of showing the world who we are, and who we hope to be one day, when we get promoted to the job of which we have long dreamed, in between all our more pressing sexual fantasies.

But then men hit the age of fifty and things start to go wrong. When I was fifty most of my friends of my age were in full-time and often well-paid jobs. Ten years later, very few of them are. It has been carnage out there.

A was a senior civil servant who fell out disastrously with his new boss, whom he described as 'a bully, a manipulator and a psychopath'. After he got chest pains and found himself weeping on the way to work one morning, he threw in the towel, just before his fiftieth birthday. 'I have never had full employment since. But I've never had so much fun either, even if I am much poorer.'

B trained as an accountant, then worked in corporate finance for many years, achieving partnership in his mid-thirties. Aged fifty-three, he had just completed a four-year term in a senior management role, and was offered something similar but less interesting. Fortunately, he says, 'fifty-three was a magic number at my firm, because it was the age from which the firm would offer long-serving partners the option of taking early retirement with a generous financial arrange-ment'. At the time I got the distinct impression he was rather disappointed by what had occurred, but he subsequently took on some non-executive roles on the boards of companies, and pro bono trustee roles on the boards of charities, 'which have enabled me to work part-time – approximately three days per week – leaving me with a great deal more leisure time to frit-ter away on idle pursuits'. (Such as long pub lunches with me.)

After a long career as a journalist, C was working in PR for a large company we can't mention, who operate in a field we also can't mention, because C has signed a non-disclosure agreement. He too was undermined by a colleague, and edged out at the age of fifty-three and a half. His wife still works, and would rather he got himself a proper job, but he is happy cooking, reading and playing golf, and now looks ten years younger than he did in the last terrible days of his terrible job.

D had worked in the City for many years and by his early fifties had fetched up at a Japanese bank, where he was working in equity capital markets. But his boss turned out to be 'a lying bastard' and got the boot, which made the rest of the team vulnerable. As they handed D his P45, the bank cited a need to 'restructure', thanks to 'rising regulation and falling revenues'. 'For thirty-odd years,' says D, 'I had done a pressured, competitive job often calling for very long hours, but I had loved the vast majority of all I had done ... There is little doubt that infinite golf and bridge in the decade that has followed hasn't been as much fun.'

Whereas all the freelances like me are still doing what we ever did. Not quite so much of it, it is true, and for less money, but we are still in the game, just about.*

A lot of companies operate a pyramid structure, with lots and lots of junior (and cheap) employees gradually being winnowed away as they rise through the firm's hierarchy until you just get one or two people at the top, massively overcompensated, with cantilevered, hydraulically supported office chairs to cope with their ever-increasing bulk. The problem comes about two-thirds of the way up the pyramid, when people are comfortable and well paid, and don't really want to leave if they don't have to. With retirement in sight they hunker down for the last stretch, only to find that there's no actual need for them in the company, none at all. There are all sorts of ways of encouraging middle managers and senior managers to bugger off, some more brutal than others, but the message is the same. Bye-bye. Toodle-pip. Elvis has left the building.

All my young/old friends who received the boot had two things in common. One was that they weren't expecting it, even if they had long dreaded it and the signs had been there for most of them to read. 'Onward and upward' had long been their personal mission statement, and suddenly there was no

---

* On 18 June 2021, a writer called Paul Bassett Davies tweeted thus: 'Freelancers! Celebrate National Freelancers Day by running through the streets naked. There's no money in it, but it'll be great exposure for you.'

onward and there was no upward. I think it takes quite a long time to get used to this, and for many it's a form of bereavement: laying your career to rest with due ceremony. Normal bereavement legendarily has five stages, and they apply here: denial, anger, bargaining, depression and acceptance. I have seen my friends through all these stages, and in one or two cases it wasn't a pretty sight. But they all came out the other side, a sentence I write with considerable relief.

The other thing they had in common was it took them a while to realise that it wasn't just the job that had come to an end: it was work, full stop. It might seem ridiculous to chuck huge numbers of perfectly capable and experienced men of a certain age onto the scrapheap years before you have to, but this is what the corporate world does all the time. But then the corporate world doesn't have our best interests at heart. It never did. That it might have done was an illusion generated by the (often substantial) amounts of money it paid. People who are poorly paid expect the companies that employ them to shaft them, because effectively they already have, simply by paying them so badly. The well paid expect to be treated with more respect, and are often genuinely surprised when they are not.

Of course there are exceptions, and everyone is different. C, the former journalist, was intensely aggrieved that his job had gone – because he had lost the battle and the war – but not particularly bothered that work itself had gone too. He had been dreaming of retirement since his mid-twenties. For him, profound inactivity had long been a serious career goal.

Ten years ago I wrote about the purging of ambition, one of the most satisfying symptoms of middle age, and one of the least expected. I realise now that, at fifty, this process was only just starting, while at sixty it is pretty much complete. All that scurrying around for personal advantage, and to what end? What seemed compulsory in our twenties, and an act of increasing desperation in our forties, now starts to look like a symptom of mental illness. If you are still attempting to climb the greasy pole in your sixties, you will have noticed that there is more grease on it than ever before, and that it only goes up a certain way, maybe a few feet. Whereas before it reached high into the sky, well beyond sight, up into the clouds and probably interfering with the flight path. The only young/oldies who still want to climb higher are those who have climbed quite high already. If you have been Foreign Secretary, you will really want to be Prime Minister. If you have been Director-General of the BBC, you will really want to run the Royal Opera House. The rest of us have come to our senses.

The purging of ambition, I believe, is one of the most beautiful things that can happen to a human being. (People who have been purged of sexual desire say much the same thing, but for some reason I find that harder to believe.) The need to make a mark, make a name for yourself, was once extremely real, and for many of us was the highest-octane fuel in our engines. My friend M has never had any ambition at all, literally none, and for many years considered himself almost disabled. All he ever wanted was a quiet life, which as it happens he didn't get (but that's another story). All he asked from a job was that it would keep him amused and entertained, for the enemy was not other people (as most ambitious people believe) but boredom. As a result he has slightly drifted through life, irked by his own passivity, but

I keep telling him that that is who he is and it's no better or worse than anything else. To live an authentic life is what we would all like to do, or say we would like to do, but M is one of few who has actually done it. If he could only pluck up the courage to leave his wife (which he never will), I think he might find his retirement quite enjoyable.

The enemy now is boredom. D, the former banker, plays bridge and golf to fill his days, not out of any passion for bridge or golf. He is the only one of my friends who genuinely misses his job. Everybody else seems quietly attuned to lower activity levels. I have another friend, whom we shall call E, who was a high-powered management consultant in charge of a large team. Then, at the age of fifty-five, he had a small stroke, from which, luckily, he has made an almost complete recovery. But his voice is more quivery these days; and occasionally he can't remember the word for 'table' or some such; and he is a far less dominant personality, much quieter and more ruminative than before. And these tiny changes have actually made it impossible for him to carry on doing his job. 'Do you miss it?' I asked him. 'No,' said E with a sly grin.

The enemy is boredom for us all. Do I want to do this job that I have been doing for years even though it bores me to death? No I don't. Being interested and engaged in what you are doing becomes more important than anything. When we were ambitious we were willing to be bored because we knew that may be the price we had to pay to reach the next stage in our precious careers. But as ambition recedes, boredom hardens into inertia. If I can just keep doing this dreary job for a few more years, the thinking goes, then I can retire and I will be free. This isn't living. This is subsisting. It's amazing how many people endure tedious jobs for years, then finally retire and are then instantly run over by runaway trucks or eaten by wolves on a day's walk in the countryside.

The real problem with ambition is that it's not much fun. When I was younger I was tirelessly ambitious and, like all ambitious people, completely self-absorbed. If someone I thought was talentless was given a newspaper column I had had my eye on, my rage and envy knew no bounds. So who gained from that, exactly? No one. Who lost? Only me. It was a complete waste of time and energy.

Several of my friends, both male and female, went through a harsh stage, which usually coincided with their most successful (and therefore most stressful) years. In a harsh stage, you don't smile as much as you used to. Charm is *de trop*. To show your mettle you have to be decisive, matter-of-fact, businesslike at all times. In short, you have to be harsh. It's a harsh world out there, and if you're not harsh enough, someone else will be harsher.

I saw this in a few people and in every case I thought it was a permanent change. But it never was. Sooner or later ambition was purged, either by circumstance or by the passing years. The harsh gradually ceased to be harsh, relaxed, smiled again, looked younger than they had for a long time. The sun came out, blossoms budded on trees, heavenly choirs burst into song on every street corner.

(Actually, there was one man who never came back from his harsh stage. But it took me a while to work out that the harsh stage wasn't, for him, a passing phase, it was his true personality. He had been concealing it under a carapace of hail-fellow-well-met jollity for decades, an enormous psychological burden that just became too much for him to bear. So he reverted to who he really was: an angry, bitter little man who cheated on all his girlfriends, lied to everyone about everything and, once rumbled, disappeared from all our lives with a slightly satanic puff of purple smoke. Some have said that he has done the decent thing, although throwing himself off Beachy Head would have been decenter.)

The passing of ambition is an excuse, if you needed one, to sue for peace with the world, and possibly with your loved ones. It really depends on whether you have come through your midlife crisis relatively unscathed. More than a few men wake up one morning, remember they have left their wives and children for a younger woman who has never even heard of Morecambe and Wise, and realise that they have utterly cocked things up. But all this is for a later chapter.

5

Youth

Finally picking up *A Shed of One's Own* and leafing through its now curled and foxed pages, I realise that at the age of fifty we were all obsessed with the younger generation, whom we had identified as the main threat to both our present and our future. Young people were (i) bright-eyed, (ii) bushy-tailed, and (iii) had a lean and hungry look, as though they wanted to eat us rather than be us. Or maybe it was just our careers they wanted to feast on. They all had the latest mobile phones and could operate with unbecoming ease the seventy-three different remote controls needed for even the simplest tele-vision set. They spoke a different language, or possibly several different languages, with an innate understanding of text-speak and emojis, and any attempts on our part to keep up with their new slang and beard preferences were seen for what they were: desperate pedalling by a soon-to-be-forgotten generation of old farts. The real problem was jealousy. These young pups had full heads of hair and their own terrible music, and they were all going out with the young women we thought we should be going out with, if we weren't manacled to a partner of roughly our own age who knew what our secrets were and where the money was and weren't planning to relinquish either any time soon.

But let's look at it another way. Ten years ago was not a particularly good time to be young. Now may be even worse. Climate change, Covid-19, Brexit (mainly voted for by the old and the half-witted), the fragility of employment, the impossibility of ever being able to buy a house unless your parents are multi-millionaires – you wouldn't wish these on anyone, and they are problems we simply didn't have to deal with when we were their age. So much has changed for the worse since we were in our twenties, although I'll grant you that the clothes are better, and pub food has improved beyond all imagination. But yesterday, as I wrote this, Vladimir Putin invaded Ukraine, and my mother rang up in a terrible tizzy, concerned that her grandsons would be con- scripted into the army and forced to go and fight Russians in the trenches outside Kyiv. I told her this was about as likely as her being conscripted, with her silly little dog to be used as a company mascot, before finally being eaten by starving soldiers on the frontlines. 'Oh no, don't say that,' she said, believing as she does that saying something makes it more likely to happen in real life, rather than less likely, as is usually the case. I was able to reassure her that her three grandsons were completely safe from such a fate, although being blown up in a nuclear fireball wasn't entirely out of the question.

But I digress. The young are very clear about where the blame lies for this parlous state of affairs: with us, their elders, the 'baby boomers'. Millennials blame boomers for everything, although it would probably be fairer to say that we have benefited from a series of economic advantages that are simply no longer available. Free university education, an NHS unburdened by huge debt, staff shortages and a hostile government, a property market that made it possible for me to buy a flat in north London in 1988, a flat that is now worth six times what I paid for it, even though it remains small and undistinguished. Millennial friends of mine are always going on about how greedy, lazy and entitled boomers are. But I'm a boomer, I say. No you're not, they reply, you may be the same age as them but at heart you're one of us. What, I'm skint and I spend what little money I have on alcohol? That would do it, they say. Oddly enough, the three adjectives millennials use of boomers are exactly the same adjectives boomers use of millennials: greedy, lazy and entitled. They may both be right, which suggests that in its essence humanity never really changes at all.

Besides, the young people we were fretting about ten years ago are young no longer. They may have our jobs and our cars and the women we fancied, but they are now looking over their shoulders at the generation younger than them, who have the hungry eyes they used to have. Swings and roundabouts, kids, swings and roundabouts. You're only up for so long before it all comes crashing down, and you too are compelled to waste your days playing bridge with octogenarians, or forced out onto the golf course in terrible sweaters in all kinds of weather, like glorious sunshine.

I'm not sure I feel so strongly about young people any more, other than enjoying their company probably more than is entirely dignified. My friend, the columnist, critic and louche man about town Nick Lezard, is a big fan of the young, and he says they instinctively gravitate to young/

oldies like him who are in unceasing rebellion against adult-hood. I am sure he is right, and it's one reason I have young friends as well. (Another is that they are much nicer to look at than the old gits.) One secret is not to dislike them for anything that they can do and you can't. Does it truly matter if you have no idea how to get Netflix on the television, if you have a teenager lying around who can do it for you? I would say not. I think they also like my quaint old-fashioned habits, like not owning a mobile phone and preferring to pay with cash if at all possible. It all comes from a longstanding aversion to doing what the Man, or indeed anyone else, wants me to do. Nick also smokes like a beagle and drinks like a fish, preferring a notably rough Chilean red from Majestic purely because it's ridiculously cheap. It's so cheap that once you take off the tax you pay on every bottle of wine, they're pretty much paying you to drink it. I'm sure Nick would drink £100 bottles of wine if he could, probably with indecent haste, but needs must, and if they are almost paying you to drink their disgusting wine, he feels it would be rude to refuse.

At a recent lunch my friend G was staring off into the distance and saying, 'I know I am sixty-two and I certainly look sixty-two, but here, in my heart of hearts [thumps chest meaningfully] I feel about twenty-seven.' I wouldn't go that far, but I would say about thirty-five for me, when I had a really cool raincoat and didn't look so bad. The important thing is not to resent the young for all the things they have that we no longer have. It's their turn, and none of those things ever last. The full head of hair will go down the plughole, and the bladder control will almost certainly fail them, as it fails so many of us, on the endless stretch between Archway and Highgate stations on the Northern line.* Their gleaming white teeth will turn brown and crumble into dust, Apple will invent something they simply don't understand (and have no wish to understand), and the luscious young lovelies on their arms will probably trade them in for someone richer and more interesting than them, who will look distressingly like Jon Hamm in *Mad Men*.

The point to remember is that we had our turn, and if we didn't make the most of it, we're like almost everyone else who has ever lived. I recently found a photo of me, aged twenty-four and a half, when I was working for a PR company and representing my dreary clients at some trade fair or other. I am wearing a cheap but not badly cut grey suit, a shirt and a tie, and I look like Roger Moore in *The Saint* (i.e. before he started wearing those godawful safari suits in the James Bond films). I am elegant, I am passably good-looking and I am probably thinking of chatting up the girl working behind the Strawberry Shortcake counter inside the stand. But I won't, because I am far too shy and timid, as I always was in those days. Opportunities lost, chances not taken, humiliations easily avoided: those were my twenties. Quite glad to have seen them off, if I am going to be perfectly honest.

'Youth is wasted on the young,' say all old people with a knowing glint, and it was certainly wasted on me. Youth is about making terrible mistakes, bad haircuts, worse clothes, disastrous facial hair decisions that we would not make now that we are older and wiser, and happier, I would say. Being old, and not having died yet, are our *rewards* for surviving

---

* I am informed that the equally brutal stretch between King's Cross St Pancras and Highbury & Islington on the Victoria line presents similar problems.

youth, not the price of it. If our bodies don't work quite as well as they did, it doesn't really matter. That was then, this is now. I have a friend – seriously, a real friend* – whose endless disappointment with his flaccid member compelled him to experiment with Viagra. And he said it was terrible. It was like being sixteen all over again, although the desire was not actually inspired by anything so alluring as a woman of the female persuasion. It just felt as though some unscrupulous surgeon had installed a titanium spine down the middle of his organ. It didn't feel a part of him, as his organ always used to. Unable to satisfy its wants and/or needs, my friend says he ended up looking back on his previous flaccidity with some fondness. Then and there he decided to retire from the sexual act altogether, and his wife having indeed run off with someone who looked distressingly like Jon Hamm in *Mad Men* was neither here nor there. A brave decision, although the fact that my friend now looks like an AI recreation of an ugly fat bloke – think John Prescott, or possibly Jabba the Hutt without the charm – probably made it slightly easier.

Let's be blunt: who of our age would genuinely want to be young again? It's OK, I'm sure, if you know what you know now but are magically made thirty years younger, but that's not the way genies in bottles operate: there's always a sting in the tail. You'd be magically thirty years younger but you would have no life experience to call upon, so would be doomed to make exactly the same mistakes you made first time around. And think how painful they were, and how foolish you felt after you had made them. In my case there were several very promising career opportunities I turned down

---

* i.e. not me.

through fear, which in such circumstances I would almost certainly turn down again, but almost all the serious regrets of my twenties and thirties involve women. Women I never pursued. Women I could have pursued but lacked the courage to. Women I pursued briefly but gave up on. Women I didn't pursue because a good friend of mine fancied them and it would be letting him down to make a play for them. (What on earth was I thinking?) Women I put on the back burner for next time, only there was no next time. (That was particularly gutless, I now realise.) One woman who invited me back to her place and I didn't go because I was playing cricket the following morning and the bloke giving me a lift was turning up at 11 a.m. Why did I say no? What kind of galloping fool was I? Another woman, who I shared a cab with one night and whom I should, if firing on all cylinders, have asked out for lunch the following week, only I didn't and the opportunity lapsed. I didn't even ask for her phone number! And that beautiful girl behind the Strawberry Shortcake counter: whatever happened to her? Can you imagine making the same terrible mistakes again? I'm afraid I can.

I don't want that lack of confidence, that shyness, that terrible crippling timidity. It has taken me thirty years to banish such feelings, or at least overpower them with regular displays of surface confidence (which do actually work). Being young is a mug's game. I'm no longer young, and I'm no longer a mug, and I don't miss either state at all.

6

Mellow or Mad?

As ambition drifts off to die, we are said by our more appreciative associates to have 'mellowed'. I am not sure I wholly like this term, implying as it does that we now only listen to Herb Alpert's Tijuana Brass and wear comfy golfing sweaters. There is a huge premium in modern society on being 'edgy', which essentially means youthful. Have you lost your edge? Were you sorry to see it go? It seems to me, though, that pure experience smooths off our edges, which more often than not are caused by the discomfort, or maybe cluelessness, of youth. When I was young I didn't have the slightest idea what was going on; now I have slightly more idea, and I would rather be me now than me then. If this is mellowing then I will take it, unruly eyebrows, tennis elbow and all.

Anyway, it's not strictly accurate, because mellow suggests becoming blander, and that's simply not true of anyone I know. What is definitely the case is that people become kinder. Those questionnaire interviews that turn up in most newspapers these days often ask 'What has life taught you?' And more often than not, the celebrity being interrogated responds with something like 'Kindness is all that matters.' And they are right. Most of my friends have become much kinder over the past ten years, and they are not afraid to show it either. If we were still rather self-absorbed at fifty, we are less so at sixty. Because we know the game is up and that time is limited, and we have also realised that kindness to others is not only good in itself, it makes us feel better too, both physically and emotionally. Instead of constantly looking inward – an unfortunate consequence of the ambitious temperament – we start to look outward. And if the vicissitudes of life have not damaged us irreparably, we often like what we see. Kindness, if you can attain that state, is wholly beneficial in every way, and I think it's only at this age that you realise this. You just have to hope that it's not too late, after all those years of behaving like a complete shit.

The only problem is that this doesn't happen to everyone. Some people do not become kinder. In fact, they seem to become more awkward, more angry, more 'edgy' with each passing year. Being young/old brings them no peace or equilibrium; it just seems to make them even more bonkers than before. A few of my friends have seriously lost the plot. One or two of them are no longer my friends. The dichotomy is so extreme that, from the outside, it looks like a conscious choice, although obviously it is anything but. Mellow, or mad? Which way are you going to go?

My former friend from a few chapters ago, the one whose harsh stage turned out to be his real personality, is the perfect example. For years he had been wearing a mask of good cheer, while gnashing his teeth with hatred and envy underneath. They say that if you wear a mask for long enough it becomes your face, but not for this fellow. For him the mask became something he hated, as much as he hated almost everyone he knew, his dead father who had beaten him like a gong and, of course, himself. The cost of his Herculean efforts to be seen as a nice person rose inexorably. Behind the scenes, it turned out, he was treating his various girlfriends with an almost casual cruelty, gaslighting them, having days-long tantrums, smoking furiously in the garden, unable to control his mounting rage. I had known him for many years and I had seen early signs of this nearly forty years ago, but I had no idea how profoundly, incurably unhappy he had become. The mask was, for many years, highly effective. It slipped only rarely. But none of his numerous former girlfriends would have anything to do with him, and most of our mutual friends had dropped him, usually after he had done something so terrible they would never talk about it. I was the last man standing, until he did something terrible to me and then I was gone too.

The cause of all this, obviously, is early trauma, never dealt with. After he had assaulted his wife and she had left him never to return, he underwent some expensive and intensive therapy, which seemed to work. For a while he was clearly happier and more balanced than he ever had been. But he needed to keep doing this for the rest of his life, not just a six-month course. The bad behaviour returned and escalated. Every relationship ended disastrously. Every friendship ended with hatred and mutual recrimination, and in my case a nine-page letter from his solicitor full of lies.

Who could be bothered to spread such chaos? But he had no choice in the matter. His wound ran deep, and as he got older it ran deeper. It could never heal and it will never heal. If you have a malignant narcissist like this in your life, the only thing you can do is set them adrift before their chaos embroils you. Unable to trust his parents, this fellow could trust no one, and thought everyone was out to do him down. In the end, of course, everyone *was* out to do him down, because he had behaved so horribly to all of them.

It's funny: there's probably no one in the world I now hate more than this man, but at the same time I feel sorry for him, for buggering things up so comprehensively. Friendships are hard won and easily trashed. Needless to say, none of it is his fault; he is always in the right; everyone else is in the wrong. His lies are actually his truth, and they need to be, for him to be able to function at all.

A friend of a friend is a horrible drunk. Amiable and sweet-natured when sober – not least because he feels so guilty about how awful he has been when drunk – he becomes a monster when alcohol has been consumed. Dr Jekyll + gargle = Mr Hyde. He is violent, foul-mouthed and, for a young/oldie not in the best of shape, genuinely terrifying because he has no inhibitions, and he has a direct line to all the rage he normally manages to quell. He has been barred from all the pubs in a remarkably wide radius of his house, and he doesn't have a lot of teeth left because they have been knocked out in fights. If I meet him at a party I check, as everyone does, that he is drinking tonic water; otherwise you really want to be somewhere else, as soon as possible. How his wife puts up with it, no one knows.

On Father's Day, on social media, he put up a picture of himself as a small boy holding his father's hand. His father looked sullen and menacing. The caption went something along the lines of the following (from memory, as the post was deleted very quickly): 'Happy Father's Day to all my friends. Unfortunately my own father was a bully and a tyrant and should never have been allowed within thirty feet of parenthood.'

Ah, right, I thought, now I understand.

In his book *They F*** You Up*, the psychologist Oliver James explains that the earlier the trauma in a child's life, the harder it is to eradicate. If you are grievously emotionally wounded within the first six weeks of your life, the chances are that you will never get over it, however much therapy you do. From six weeks to six months, the wounds run less deep, and if something horrible happens to you between six months and six years you might actually be able to eradicate its effects, if you feel so inclined. But if you are terrorised throughout childhood by a villainous, tyrannical, self-centred and occasionally violent father, you may well be hanging on by your fingertips for the rest of your life.

The malignant narcissist thinks only of himself, and everything revolves around his ceaseless emotional pain. At his core there is a void where there really shouldn't be. Some pour drink into that void, others hoover up drugs, some smoke themselves into the middle of next week, others shag everything that moves, but nothing works. Nothing *can* work. Some seek power to make them feel whole, which explains at least one recent prime minister of the UK and at least one president of the United States, but even power is a disappointment. Imagine power being a disappointment! But it's like an amputee trying desperately to grow a leg back. At least genuine amputees know that's never going to happen.

You can also see why people who start off slightly mad have, by the age of sixty, gone full whipcrack tonto, as dangerous to themselves as they are to other people, and they are pretty damn dangerous to other people. My former friend did not *set out* to lose every old friend he had ever had, although there seems an inevitability now to the way events unfolded. For madness is the very opposite of control: its sworn enemy, if you prefer. It strikes me as revealing that in all his relationships he sets out to control his girlfriends as rigidly as possible, possibly because most of the time he is unable to control himself at all.

I myself had a father who was bullying, tyrannical, emotionally cauterised and borderline psychopathic, so why am I not a basket case as well?

(*looks searchingly in the mirror for a moment*)

Actually, I think I was lucky. I was the first child (we think), my father and mother were most in love in my early years, and my father apparently only gets tired of his children when they reach five or six, which certainly happened to me: I can remember the sudden withdrawal of affection like a gunshot. But my first few years were blissfully happy and I was much loved. And when my father moved on, all too briefly, to my younger brother, my mother gave me all the love I needed and more. I never felt the lack of my father's love because it rapidly became clear that he didn't really love anyone other than himself. When he finally ran off with the spotty, heavy-calved Polish au pair when I was fourteen, I was glad to see him go, unlike my mother and brother, who were heartbroken.

For forty years I have run a grotty travelling cricket team, who regard it as a triumph of World Cup-winning proportions if they record more than two victories in a season. As well as generously providing me with the material for my first book (*Rain Men*, 1995) and my fourth book (*Zimmer Men*, 2005), they have also taught me many, many lessons on the ways of men and how they behave in the company of other men, especially in the dressing room, where I have learned to my abject horror how late-middle-aged men look when they take their clothes off. For we have aged together. Several have retired, crocked by injury, or just disadvantaged by general wear and tear, and they have usually been replaced by very slightly younger people, although at the moment we do have two wicketkeepers in their early seventies who play every game as though it might be their last, because realistically it might be. Many of these players I have known for twenty years, a few for thirty years, one or two for forty years. I think that running this team might be one of the proudest achievements of my life.

But where do they all stand on the mellow/mad scale? There is no question that many of them have mellowed remarkably. The years have stilled their rage. Quite a lot of the team just appreciate each other more, are pleased when someone does well. One of the main gags in *Rain Men*, which was written at the height of my team's internecine strife, was that players were so busy competing with their teammates they almost forgot about the opposition. Which was true at the time, as all good jokes have to be. Now there's genuine camaraderie, and it's a lovely thing to see.

And one reason for this is that, gradually, all the madder players have disappeared. We had a couple of players who, I suspect, were on the Asperger spectrum: not autistic, but somewhere in the foothills of the condition. They were actually both very kind men, but it was as though neither of them quite spoke human, which has been the defining quality of all the people with autism I have known. One of them, a cricketing obsessive, was the single most selfish player I have encountered, and there have been quite a few candidates for that lofty status. His neediness was in inverse proportion to his actual cricketing skills, and everyone who captained the team spent much too much of their time and energy having to deal with him and his endless requirements. In his last season he took four catches and topped the catches league, which he had never done before. But he had also dropped at least twenty, because the ball unerringly found him, wherever anyone tried to hide him in the field, as though it had a guidance system. When he left he did so in an explosion of recriminations and accusations: he unfriended me on Facebook and has never spoken to me again. A year or two later he wondered why he was no longer on the team's email distribution list. I heard he took up the ukulele. The team improved instantaneously for his absence.

Another player, only in his early forties, took against the most amiable of his teammates, wrote poisonous emails about this entirely innocent man and vanished overnight. A third, a spiky and loquacious character, was bowling his pies to a decent young batsman and being smashed to all parts. Unfortunately he chose to vent his rage on the umpire, who may have been a career criminal in his spare time, or at the very least a highly successful bouncer. Our player, clearly outgunned, stomped off the field, got in his car, drove home and never played again.

But if you had asked me five years ago whether these three players would all vanish from our lives, I would have laughed in your face. The first two went madder than I had thought possible, and the third was always pretty bonkers but, I believed, relatively stable. The point is that we become who we were always going to be, but no one, least of all ourselves, has much clue who that is going to be. It's the adventure of life, I suppose, although some might see it more as an obstacle race with some really brutal obstacles. The pits get deeper and wider as you move through the course, the ladders to escape from them disappear, and there are hungry leopards at the bottom of the most distant few. You could probably get the blindfold off, if you didn't have both arms tied behind your back.

7

Friends

Four or five years ago, in a whimsical moment, a group of not-quite-as-employed-as-they-used-to-be friends and I formed a small club, which we called WALLS: the Wednesday Afternoon Long Lunch Society. We meet once a month in a pub at about 1 p.m. We eat, we drink, we talk drivel, and if it's the summer and we are out of doors, we stare at passing girls. After five or six hours of this, we stagger to our various homes, pass out and snore like lawnmowers. It is as utterly and straightforwardly enjoyable as anything you can imagine.

I have told other friends about WALLS and their usual response is (a) can I come? and/or (b) I would love to do something like that.

To which the answers are (a) no* and (b) why don't you? What's stopping you?

I have written in previous books, probably too often, of the pleasures of the long lunch, which are grievously underrated

---

* We have decided that six is the perfect number, and that there will be no vacancies until one of us croaks. And when you see how fat some of us are getting, that day may not be too far away . . .

by modern capitalistic society, which generally favours a sandwich at your desk and maybe a Cadbury's Twirl for afters. What joyless lives people lead. When you are young and driven and keen to suck up to whoever is in charge, I can see the appeal of the swift lunch-snack and back to work, staring at your computer as though you're afraid it's going to leap off your desk and run away. But we are now sixty, for fuck's sake. When does thankless toil end and pleasure begin? If not now, when? as Primo Levi once wrote, possibly about something else.

Personally, I think it's a little sad that so many of us can only let our hair down after most of that hair has departed, but the past is gone and there's nothing we can do about that. Unless you got so drunk you danced on the table or tried to fondle someone, no one has ever regretted a long lunch, in the way that no one in the history of the world has ever said, I wish I hadn't gone on that holiday, I could have got so much more work done if I had stayed at home.

WALLS works because there are only six of us, and we have all known each other for thirty years. As old friends tend to be, we are all quite similar: very verbal, tending towards drollery, but in truth quite quiet and not naturally disposed to dominate the conversation. No one has anything to prove, each of us has his quirks, and everyone else respects those quirks. Quite a lot of what I have written about in this book started as a conversation at WALLS. Not that I have been taking notes, you understand, and there is the problem that you will remember very little that happens after three o'clock, owing to beer.

The value of friends is something you have to discover for yourself, and men can be catastrophically bad at keeping up with each other, for all sorts of reasons. One problem is the hermit tendency, which I wrote about ten years ago, and which still applies. Most women I know have huge networks of friends they carefully nurture, while their menfolk sit in their sheds by themselves, listening to *Test Match Special* on the radio. I have known a few men who realised, in their forties and fifties, that they simply didn't have any friends at all. They didn't think they needed them, until they did. They were too busy working. Maybe they relied too much on the family unit, which can be very seductive. Maybe there were cars to wash, DIY to botch, sofas to fall asleep on. Maybe people moved away, or grew apart, or grew apart and moved away. At the top of my road there used to be a wonderful old pub full of solitary middle-aged (and older) men nursing their pints and saying nothing to anyone.* Occasionally one of them would die and a photo of him would be put up behind the bar with a black border. A new solitary man would take his stool and life would carry on as before.

I too have started to go to pubs by myself with a book, not to speak to anyone but simply to be alone in company, which for some reason I find very relaxing. I didn't do this five years ago, and now I do it most days of the week, rarely for more than half an hour or forty-five minutes, and alternating between all the different pubs in my area. Does old-man behaviour creep up on us like this? I understand that my own craving for solitude is fairly extreme, given that my family and I all live in a small flat that often feels even smaller than it is. But this doesn't seem like a solution

---

* Miraculously this pub has recently reopened, after seven years' closure. It's exactly as it was, if not better (because both of my children work there) and I pop in for a swift one most days.

a young man would choose. A young man wouldn't sigh with pleasure as he takes his first sip and contemplates the next three-quarters of an hour, in which he will say not a single word to anyone.

Silence.

The joy of no conversation.

No talking and, even better, no listening.

Just time alone with your own thoughts.

And, if you manage to attain a state of pub nirvana, no thoughts at all.

I don't think I realised until very recently how much people talk, and what bilge most of it is. My beloved partner, who has many fine attributes, never stops talking, and my son and my daughter have inherited it from her. Fortunately, when they are all together, they can all talk to each other, while I go and hide in my office and put loud music on. My partner, I have realised, thinks through talking. If she has a problem, she likes to talk it through until it is solved. Whereas I prefer to think through thinking, which often includes long walks by myself, when so many of life's most knotty problems are quickly solved. My mother, whose endless nattering should really have been put to more practical use, like generating electricity for the nation, rings me up and talks to me for five minutes, and then talks to Polly for an hour. When I was a teenager I would talk on the phone to my friends for an hour, maybe even two. Now the mere idea of doing this fills me with a visceral horror I usually only experience when I have an imminent dental appointment. What on earth do they have to say to each other? The fact is, it doesn't matter what they have to say to each other, it's the act of saying it that gives them the pleasure.

I am quite sociable, though, and when I see my friends I obviously talk and listen to them like a normal person. What is it about the endless blathering of family members that drives me up the wall? I know I am not alone in this. A lot of men of my age say the same thing. The conversations of friends: informative, illuminating, enjoyable. The conversation of family members: completely maddening. It does seem to be one of the mysteries of life.*

Friends come and friends go. I have recently been sidelined by a friend of thirty-five years' standing because, I think, she just got tired of me. Which is fair enough: I get tired of me, for god's sake. And with some friends the conversation simply runs out. I had a good friend, not a particularly close friend, Championship level rather than Premier League, who lives near me, used to be part of my pub quiz team, but one day there was just nothing more to say to one another, literally nothing. We would bump into each other at parties and both our minds would go blank. A while ago I was in the pub with some other friends and I spotted this character on the other side of the bar with another friend of his. I went over and said hello and then stood there with nothing to say, as he sat there with nothing to say either. Weird. No malice, no hostility. Just nothing.

But our tastes change, in people as in everything else.

---

* Actually, I think repetition might be the key. When my mother starts on one of her stories, I think, Have I heard this ten times before, or twenty-five times, or even fifty? And as she tells it again, I wish that a bell would ring for the hundredth repetition of a much-loved anecdote. Maybe she should get a little prize. By extraordinary coincidence I turn out to be her son. My partner claims that she has heard literally everything I have to say more times than she can bear.

Most of the new friends I have made over the past fifteen years have been women – no, not for that reason, but because they are so much more interesting than most men. I have often wondered about this. Is this just my heterosexuality talking? (Possibly.) Is this because I was brought up by a woman to whom I am still very close, even though she drives me mental quite a lot of the time? (Very possibly.) Or is it just because, with my tastes changing, with me becoming the person I was always going to be, I now find a lot of men rather boring?

My friend Russell, who also has more female friends than male friends, has a wonderful line on the terrible limits of male conversation. He says they only really have three subjects: sport, work and machines (by which he means cars, computers and the like). I laughed when he told me this, but I didn't quite believe him. No, he said, the next time you are in the pub with your book, just listen. Identify the nearest group of men and eavesdrop. So I did. And he's right. Not entirely right, but very much more right than he has any right to be.

We should never underestimate the power of obsession. Many men think their extremely boring hobbies are of interest not just to themselves but to all other men, and this is the fourth subject of male conversation. There is a bloke in the pub who would always talk to me about comics, because he knew I liked *Star Trek* and presumed, from that, that I would be fascinated by Batman, Superman and the like. But I'm not. 'I don't like comics. I never read comics,' I would tell him over and over again, and he would look at me in complete mystification. It took him *eighteen months* of these occasional conversations to fully comprehend what I was trying to say and stop talking to me about bloody comics.

I would say, though, that as I have found more female friends, so I have increasingly lost patience with my older male friends with Aspergic tendencies. There's clearly a connection between the two, and I think it's empathy. The women have it, the men do not. The problem has probably come about because I hang around in quiz circles, and an awful lot of the best quizzers, you will be astonished to hear, are somewhere on the spectrum. They are some of the most competitive people you could ever meet. They rarely smile, they lack charm (in the same way that they lack a third leg) and they never say thank you. After a while the company of such men begins to pall. I generally run screaming if any of them even enters the room.

Of course, you could point out that it's not very empathetic of me to have so little empathy for the unempathetic, and you would be right.

But this is a shift for me and while I can't explain it, I can certainly try to understand it. As I said in the introduction, 'a lot of us think of ourselves as serenely unchanging, as beacons of consistency in an uncertain world', but change isn't just a part of life, it *is* life. Forty years ago, when I was at university, there was only one self-declared gay boy in my college. (Who later came out as Jewish, and is now a rabbi.) One out of three hundred? Even at the time I thought this was a little on the low side. As it happens many, many boys later came out as gay, and one or two of the (thirty-odd) girls did too.

But my friend Lucy, who went to the same university ten years later, said that half the people she knew in her college were gay and out, so attitudes to homosexuality had changed completely in less time than Margaret Thatcher was prime minister. Oddly enough she was prime minister at the time, so she may have had something to do with it.*

What is interesting about WALLS is that when we meet once a month, we are genuinely delighted to see each other and not afraid to show it. Such is the perilously low standard of male social intercourse that this still comes as a pleasant surprise to me, but I think most of my male friends are more empathetic than they used to be and seek empathy from others more than they did. It could just be a function of age. People are starting to die and if we don't show our friends we love them now, we may never get the chance in the future. Maybe it's our own mortality, lingering in the shadows. Maybe we have just mellowed, as others have gone mad. But most of my significant male friendships are in a better state now than they have ever been, and I can't tell you how pleased I am about this, not least because it seems to have been a natural process, without any conscious effort on my part or anyone else's.

The main realisation of this time in our lives is that there is only now. Yesterday has gone for ever, and tomorrow might not be quite so much fun. Philosophers, who often know a thing or two, have long advised their pupils to live in the present, but it's only now that circumstance compels us to do this very thing. Now is all we know that we have. Mine's a pint of Pravha, and a packet of cheese-and-onion crisps.

---

* The equivalent now would be the increasing prominence of trans people. Something we had barely heard of when we were young – although I did read Jan Morris's magnificent *Conundrum* when I was a mere teen – whereas now, according to someone who knows and told my friend Tallulah, there are at least ten boys at Eton currently transitioning into girls.

8

Money

It's probably fair to say that those of us rising sixty are the fag end of the luckiest generation of Britons there has ever been.

Baby boomers, for such are we, copped the lot. Free health-care, free university education, longer lives, some really good music and, best of all, absurdly rising wealth at just the right moment for us to make the most of it. As I mentioned earlier, my flat in north London is small and unimpressive, and has seemed ever smaller since my partner Polly moved in and we had two children, both now enormous. But if Polly and I were hacked down by a mad axeman tomorrow, our children would each inherit not enough for them to buy any sort of property in the south-east of England. This is because, aside from the flat, I don't have any money at all.

In London, being a paup is relatively unusual. (No wonder the rest of the country hates us so.) Many of my friends have serious money, and very few inherited it. A friend of mine went into the City in the early 1980s and flourished. After he had a fling with a female colleague on an overseas trip, his wife chucked him out of their substantial house in Kensington and he was compelled to buy a flat in Notting Hill. When she divorced him, she got £4.3 million, and he was left with £4.2 million, which I am sure he has cleverly expanded since because he is very good with money. But how does anyone make such sums in the first place? I simply don't know. I walk around the streets of Highgate gawping into people's windows and wonder, How did you make enough money to buy this amazing house? How do you have so much that you can afford to have bought yourself a new car and your wife a new car and given the four-year-old runabout to your teenage daughter? It's an absolute mystery to me.

Admittedly I have spent my life not in an office shouting at underlings, but in a small room writing things like this. I chose this life, or rather, it chose me, and I have no regrets. I am also not an envious person, so it worries me not at all that I am completely skint and have been for as many years as I can remember. If I am going to be scrupulously honest, I shall admit that I am not interested in money at all. But I am possibly excessively interested in my personal freedom, which I have guarded assiduously for years. It's a classic quid pro quo. Here's your personal freedom, the world is saying to me, but in return a larger-than-normal electricity bill will send you down into the pits of despair.

Climbing the corporate ladder, by contrast, does appear to bring in piles of cash; in some cases, more than you can helpfully spend on anything. I remember a party held twenty, maybe twenty-five years ago, at which I knew three couples. One was hosting the party and they were both in well-remunerated corporate jobs. Another pair were also doing pretty well, but the third were as skint as I was (he worked for the civil service and she was a teacher). The two rich couples had only one subject of conversation, which was how rich they were. At one point the men spent twenty minutes out-holidaying each other, while the women discussed home improvements. I wondered if they would start digging out their credit card slips to show each other how much they were spending. The other paup couple and I stood in the corner in silence. We had nothing to contribute to such a conversation, and I remember leaving the party in a state of simmering rage that probably took several years to abate.

(As it happens, both rich couples have since experienced serious reverses in their fortunes, and, possibly coincidentally, are much nicer than they used to be. But then, as previously discussed, most people are much nicer than they used to be, for all sorts of reasons.)

I have another friend who is swimming in funds. When we go out for dinner he tends to choose where we go, and he has expensive tastes. Fortunately he always pays for the whole thing. He is also a rather guarded character, but once he drank slightly too much red wine and revealed, in his cups, that he was dead jealous of a mutual friend of ours, who has even more money than he does. I have no idea how much, but at a guess I would say that Rich Man #1 is worth about £15 million, and Rich Man #2 about £25 million. More, in short, than either of them is ever going to spend on anything, unless they feel like buying an island. Additionally, Rich Man #1 is terrified of the Labour Party, and is convinced that its senior officials could be banging on the door of his country retreat at this very moment, intending to come in, steal all his belongings and make a bonfire of them. I told him he lived in a gated community of the mind, although not until after he had bought me dinner.

How does the onset of money change a man? In many different ways. Some are generous and buy you dinner, others are skinflints. Some invite you to stay at their large and comfortable piles, others very much do not. One or two start socialising only with other rich people, possibly because this is what they have always aspired to do, and occasionally because they are no longer wholly comfortable with poor people. We tend not to have dinner parties for entirely practical reasons (dining table the size of a postage stamp etc.) but also because we once invited a rich couple for dinner who were clearly embarrassed to be there, perched awkwardly on our saggy old sofa and wondering why they had driven all this way only to eat the best fish pie they will ever have eaten anywhere. I don't mind being poor, but I do slightly resent other people minding our being poor. They don't have to do it. It is we who have taken on the burden of being broke, owing only to a chronic lack of funds.

Wealth makes some men mellow and other men mad. One or two I know believe that money has made them morally superior, or maybe that their innate moral superiority has been rewarded with lots of lovely money. Not many of them talk about luck, and a fair few will tell me repeatedly how hard they worked for their cash, which they seem to think is much harder than I worked for mine. But others really settle into their prosperity. I have a very old friend who used to work in the City and made a fortune there. He was a sharp operator who didn't care whom he upset, which is certainly one way of doing it. After he retired, his wife told me, it took him three years to calm down and become a normal person again. He is a lovely bloke now, kind and unfailingly generous, not missing his past career at all, in fact seeing it as a necessary evil to get to where he is today: happy, idle and completely loaded.

I had a decent income for most of the 1990s, when I was a single man, but I was undone by that occupational hazard of the freelance writer: two or three years when I earned much less than usual. Soon after that I started procreating, and as the years passed my debts started to mount up. By 2016 it was costing me more than £3,000 a month simply to service those debts, a sum I very rarely earned. Everything in my life was geared towards the maximisation of income. I would wake most mornings at about five o'clock and lie in bed worrying about money. Then something totally unexpected happened. One of my best friends, Chris, died what now seems ridiculously young (sixty-six) without a family, a terrible loss to me, but he left me some cash, enough to let me pay off the most expensive of those debts, which meant that the money I was making from work could start to pay off the debts that remained. I no longer wake at five in the morning, unless I desperately need a pee.

So I know from brutal experience that the possession of money makes only one substantial difference to your life: it stops you worrying about money. The poor think of nothing else. You are constantly aware that you are, at the very least, three or four minor disasters away from oblivion. What if my credit cards are maxed out and the computer blows a fuse? What would I work on? We have always had a car, which was essential when the kids were little, less so now, but none ever had a subsequent owner. Every single one was sold for scrap. Three of them were given to us by generous friends or parents. If the car broke down and needed, say, £750 spent on it, you would first think, Do I have £750, or can I borrow it from someone I haven't borrowed from before? And then you would think, Is it worth it? How long will this car last? Where is the next creaking old jalopy coming from? And so on.

In the summer of 2015, a few months before Chris died, I received a gas bill for £1,196.95, for the previous month. The 2014 bill for the same period had been £101.38, and that had been for a quarter. I went into a tailspin. Obviously I didn't have that kind of money, and even more obviously there had been a mistake: either there had been a gas leak or our meter had gone bonkers. I phoned British Gas, and after the usual four-hour wait got on to a man who listened carefully to my rising panic and told me that I could pay £101, as in the previous year, and they would investigate the matter. Two days later I received a letter from British Gas threatening me with various measures if I did not pay the remainder I 'owed'. 'If we have to visit your property to collect this debt we will charge you an additional £36,' the letter continued. 'If the debt remains unpaid we plan to obtain a court warrant to visit your home and exchange your current meter for a pre-payment meter. This could result in additional charges of up to £206, consisting of £56 for the warrant application and up to £150 for a meter exchange.' It has never been more expensive to be poor.

The matter took weeks to resolve and probably aged me ten years. It was a gas-meter fault, and it was relatively simple to spot, as the little dial was going round and round at about forty times the normal speed even though it was high summer and we were using no gas at all. But what particularly galled me was the attitude of British Gas. They simply would not admit liability. It was all down to me, until they were able to prove to their satisfaction that it wasn't. I was clearly a master criminal, guilty of fiddling with my gas meter in order to make a frivolous and fraudulent complaint. I did actually ask one of the men I spoke to, In what universe would I fake this? And why? After it was all sorted out, without further payment on my part, British Gas then refused to say sorry. I asked for an apology and the man on the end of the phone blustered abjectly. They obviously didn't have a paragraph on penitence in the script he was using.

My point is that if I had had the £1,200, I would have paid up, sorted it out later and not gone to the enormous effort of ageing ten years.

All these small and unpleasant experiences affect the body at a molecular level, which is why poor people live shorter lives: not only must their bodies absorb the physical consequences of poverty, they must absorb the stress of it too. I have never been *that* poor: we all ate and we all had a home. This is a smaller, more bourgeois form of poverty, and the suffering was smaller and more bourgeois as well. And there was, magnificently and apparently randomly, a solution. I still don't have any money, but I no longer feel quite so poor, and I can't begin to tell you how wonderful that is.

I used to wonder whether even relative poverty put its stamp upon you, changed you for ever. If you were poor as a child, say, would that wound have healed by the time you were sixty? I thought probably not, but I'm no longer sure I was right. I have two friends who have radically opposing views about money, and they bicker all the time. One is excessively cautious. He has retired with a comfortable pension and he and his wife live in a large detached house. He has money but he worries incessantly that he is going to lose it somehow, that his pension will fail, that they will have to sell the house and move into a smaller property, which for him would be the ultimate humiliation. The other is completely devil-may-care, invests aggressively, has made and lost substantial sums and regards my other friend's ceaseless fretting with mystification, if not mild disgust. So which of these two grew up in a council house with his single-parent mother, and which in solid middle-class respectability?

You've guessed it. The devil-may-care character grew up in borderline poverty, while the fretful porpentine did not.

Maybe it's the opposite of what you would think. Maybe the person who has had money all his life worries about losing it, and the person who never had it knows that life goes on without it and it's of no real importance. Or maybe it's just temperament, and there's no meaningful link with past experience at all.

We all become who we were going to be. We had no idea of who that was going to be when we were younger, and every time we look in the mirror we realise we still don't know. And there's not a lot of time left to find out.

What definitely changed for me in the paup years is that I became strangely averse to spending money. I became a skinflint, a tightwad, a mothwallet. Oh, I'll buy my round in a pub and I'll pay my share in a restaurant, but is there any real need to go on a foreign holiday this year, or indeed any year? Does anyone need more than three pairs of shoes? Do I really need to paint the outside windows of the flat as the lease demands, or shall I just spend it all on chocolate and red wine? But this is the subject of our very next chapter: Retreat.

9

Retreat

When we are young, we want to try everything. I never took any drugs – way too timid – but I did go to the opera once or twice, and may even have pretended to like it. Actually, the list of things I have never done is rather odd:

- Never smoked a cigarette.
- Never been to New York City.
- Never driven a car.
- Never worn, let alone purchased, a pair of blue jeans.

It might be more interesting to list the things I have done precisely once.

- Been on a cruise.
- Attempted to water-ski.
- Applied moisturiser.
- Gone to South Africa.
- Been a best man at a wedding. (I quite enjoyed this, so more bookings please.)

As we get older, our list of things that we do, or want to do, gets shorter and our list of things that we really don't want to do gets ever longer. I used to go to the theatre quite a lot – well, four or five times a year, which felt like a hell of a lot when you have to sit though all those plays, and no one can ever agree on whether to eat before or after, and there's all the travelling time and the incredible cost of even quite poor seats and the glass of very mediocre red wine in the interval and all the dull middle-aged and elderly people in the audience, who make you feel you have gone to the Conservative Party Conference by mistake, and the desperate, almost fevered wait for the end of the play so you can at last escape. And at some point I reached a stage at which I thought, I really don't want to do this any more. I'm a grown-up and I don't have to do it. No one can make me. Even though you are probably over fifty when this realisation hits you, you are liberated by it. The chains are unshackled. I will happily go and see a friend perform or, more usually nowadays, the grown-up child of a friend, but that's it.

In America, and even more notably in American films, there is the concept of the 'bucket list', the list of all the things ageing people want to do before they kick the bucket. Go skydiving, visit the Grand Canyon, have unprotected sex with a ladyboy in Bangkok, that kind of thing. What a waste of time. Getting older is not about embracing life's adventures, it's a slow and orderly retreat from them. It's about not doing what other people want you to do but which bores you silly. As Matt Haig said, 'Happiness occurs when you forget who you're expected to be. And what you're expected to do.' There should be only one item on the bucket list, which is 'tear up bucket list'.

When I was a teenager I was a sports nut, and would watch literally any sport on the telly, even flat racing from Doncaster and the wrestling on ITV on Saturday afternoons. My son is the same: I have spotted him, in slight desperation, watching rugby league. But gradually these sports leave us. They vanish, sport by sport. The really dull ones go first, as you might expect, and there then occurs a fundamental recalibration of your boredom-ometer. I used to be a serious Formula 1 fan, watching every single race (my son even watches qualifying sessions). But then Michael Schumacher came along and won every race, with his Teutonic efficiency and awful face. I lost interest. The same happened with golf. I would watch the dullest and least significant European Tour tournament: the Latvian Masters, say, or the Liechtenstein Open. I knew the difference between Gordon Brand Jnr and Gordon J. Brand, and could recognise them both. Then I was just watching the Majors and the Ryder Cup, and then for a number of years it was just the Ryder Cup, and now it's not even that. Generations of fake-grinning men in silly trousers have been and gone since I last watched golf. Most of my favourite players have been retired longer than they were playing.

What is this about? Is it just boredom? Or is it actually the reverse, the realisation that life has so much to offer and we have so little time in which to enjoy it that we can no longer *afford* to be bored? With sport there's the terrible repetition, and also its total godforsaken pointlessness. Once you have ceased to care which car manufacturer is winning the F1 Constructors' Championship, you will never care again.

So we retreat from dullness and obligation, and what we have left, our core interests if you like, loom ever larger in our lives. For most of us, I think this is a relief. My friend C, the retiree who cooks and reads and plays golf, is probably happier now than he has ever been: he glows with the joy of a man who knows he will be out on the course tomorrow morning, slashing his ball into the heavy rough. I have always read a lot of books, sometimes for work but mainly for pleasure, and ten years ago I was reading around fifty a year. Now it's more than a hundred. Not a conscious decision;* just a suspicion that, whenever it's sunny, I would be better off sitting in the park with a book than doing anything else at all. It's a good, sound suspicion, and I respect it.

Now, if you'll excuse me, the sun is shining and my favourite park bench is uttering its plaintive, seal-like cry.

Travel can be an awful faff. The sheer boredom of booking all your various connections, of packing most of your belongings into a tiny suitcase, of getting to the airport in time for your 7 a.m. flight, of being bodily squeezed into a tiny seat, of having to drink yourself silly to overcome your fear of flying, of the sheer brutal heat of wherever you land hitting you like a frying pan in the face, of horrible little concrete hotel rooms, of the sour din of air conditioners, of the profusion of man-eating insects, their buzzing even louder than the bloody air conditioner, of the price of a minuscule bottle of beer, of the creeping dread of returning home, of the even more depressing journey home, and of arriving home to find that you haven't actually been burgled and the house hasn't actually burned down, even though you spent the preceding

---

* Actually, this isn't true. I found the website of a fellow book critic, on which she said she read more than a hundred books a year, and I thought, Well, if she can . . .

week worrying about nothing else ... not to mention the credit card bill that assails you a couple of weeks later, when you had quietly forgotten you had ever been on holiday at all. At twenty, or thirty, or forty or even fifty, it might all have seemed worth it. At sixty, to my slight surprise, I don't go on foreign holidays at all.

This is what I mean by retreat. When you were younger you were willing to *put up* with so much. But now you have less energy and less patience. You need to conserve and focus your energy, and keep your stress levels as low as possible. I have never been to New York, not for any particular reason, other than possibly laziness, but now I can admit I don't even want to go. Everyone is appalled by this. The energy! The lights! The buzz! they all cry, not understanding that those are the three things I specifically want to avoid. If I want to relax I go for a walk in the English countryside. It costs bugger all and it feeds my soul in a way that a huge noisy city never could. Actually, I rather like European cities. Paris is magnificent, Rome is full of deranged Italians screaming at each other and Barcelona has the prettiest girls in the world. It's twenty years since I last visited any of them.

We all have different tastes and I have several friends for whom travel is still the thing. They have money and health and time, and for them every visit to an airport is still exciting and full of promise. Fine, I say. If you can maintain a Buddhist calm when security confiscate your nail scissors and Ryanair charge you to go to the loo, you are a better man than I, in every possible way. But my idea of bliss is a cottage with low ceilings in an out-of-the-way Dorset village, with a sturdy pair of walking boots, a pile of books and a pub not too far away. If this sounds to you like an old person's holiday, you would be right. We hired just such a cottage not so long ago, situated on the edge of a village next to the main path down to the sea. I'm not sure we saw a single person under fifty walk by all week.*

The retreat is an attempt to remove unnecessary complexity from our lives, to pare down, to simplify. I'm not even sure this is a conscious urge, and if it isn't, our subconscious knows something that we don't. But I do think that craving a simple life as you get older is compatible with sound mental health. Compare my father and my mother. My father lives in great luxury in the south of France, surrounded not by friends (not sure he has any) but by children and ex-wives waiting for him to die and collect their bounty. He has his first large brandy at 10 a.m., a bottle of wine at lunch, a bottle of wine at dinnertime and sundry other refreshers during the day. He has done this, my mother reckons, for at least fifty years, so he must be physically robust. There is an argument, given that he has lived so long, and that most alcoholics die young, that no one has ever drunk as much as he has, no one in the history of the world. It would be nice to be able to say that he has undertaken this existential journey on behalf of us all, but he hasn't.

My mother lives in a tiny flat at the very top of Baker Street, with a small dog, whom she takes for walks in Regent's Park.

---

* The only foreign holiday we still undertake is to go and see some writer friends who live half the year in Portugal. Their house is on a hillside in the middle of nowhere. You can see no other houses, and you can hear nothing. It can be brutally hot in the sun, but the house is cool inside, they have a swimming pool and Rob is a superb cook. It costs little more than the air fare, and I am so happy there I often think I might explode.

She has pared her life back to the essentials, which are having a nice time, buying wonderful clothes for her granddaughters and talking for Britain. I have never known anyone happier. If you offer her a second jam doughnut, she will say she really shouldn't, and then eat it anyway.

It is actually very helpful to have parents like these, one a dire warning of where self-obsession and vindictive rage will get you, the other a role model for how to live a good life. My mother does watch too many property shows on TV for my liking, but everyone has their flaws.

My own personal retreat includes the disappearance of something I am deliriously happy to see the back of: FOMO, or fear of missing out. My youth and early adulthood were blighted by this, the absolute certainty that somewhere, in some way, someone was having a much better time than I was. Were they? It probably didn't help that I wasn't a naturally youthful kind of youth. Even at the age of nineteen I preferred old men's pubs to nightclubs, and I have never been young enough to go to any sort of outdoor festival (another to add to the list). For a long, long time, I felt fatally out of kilter with most mainstream society, and it wasn't until I was much older that I realised almost everyone feels this, and that 'mainstream society', whatever that is, isn't worth a candle. Only very gradually, like an unusually tenacious virus, does FOMO leave your system. Finally it really doesn't matter what anyone else is doing. As it happens, it never mattered. It's just that you didn't know that.

FOMO is a disease of youth, even a not-very-youthful youth, and it still affects those of my contemporaries who have resisted the ageing process most stubbornly. It's a layer of anxiety that comes between you and the real world, insulating you in your misery and preventing you from seeing what is actually happening, which is just lots and lots and lots of people struggling to get by. Understanding the vulnerabilities of others – difficult to do for a young person, and often exceptionally difficult for a young male person – is the key to the cure. As FOMO retreats, you realise how much time and energy you wasted as a young person trying to be cool. This was particularly hard for me, as I was so naturally, instinctively uncool I might as well have been wearing clown trousers and falling over every twenty yards. But even if you have no gift for cool, you keep on trying. I think it's probably worse if you do have a gift for it. If you are effortlessly cool you can hide behind that carapace for ever. But then FOMO will be with you for life, and no one would wish that on their worst enemy. I now see FOMO as a motor of depression. Only when you are rid of it do you understand that it served no practical purpose whatever.

The loss of FOMO seems like a parallel process to retreat. They happen at about the same time, and possibly to the same end: living a simpler life. Once you have stopped worrying what everyone else is up to, you can concentrate on your own happiness, and, oddly enough, this takes you to other people. Many of my older friendships have become deeper and more satisfying over the past few years, as we all become more sensitive to the vulnerabilities and feelings of others, and are less afraid to show our own. Leading a simpler life, not trying to be cool, listening to others, showing kindness above all else, not doing anything you really don't want to do, always eating the second doughnut: this may not be the definitive secret to happiness, but it comes close enough for me. Of course, the fear of missing out may begin to mutate into the fear of ever doing anything at all (FOEDAAA), but that's another problem entirely.

10

Slow Down

For most of my adult life I have been the fastest walker on the pavement. No one overtook me. I was fitter, I was swifter, I was getting there first. I didn't quite break into a trot, but not far short.

And then I slowed down.

Now I amble.

Occasionally I stop completely to look at something. A notice pinned to a tree. Maybe the tree itself.

If I bump into someone I know, I stay to have a chat, whereas in the past I was always in too much of a hurry. 'Got to go!' I would yell over my shoulder.

The weirdest thing about this is that I have no idea when I made the transition from gadabout to stop-and-chat. I am glad I did, because it's a much more pleasant way to live. There's rarely any need to rush, unless you're late, and I am not often that.

Admittedly, that's when I am going somewhere by myself. For much of my life I have been going somewhere with at least one of three women. My mother has only ever had one gear, and that's slower than you can imagine. She is, and always has been, sublimely unworried about being late. As she is ninety-one, before long she will be 'the late', and she is sublimely unworried about that too.

Polly, my partner for a quarter of a century, isn't always late for everything, but that's only because I sometimes tell her the wrong time on purpose. If we have agreed to leave at 10.30 by the absolute latest, we'll get in the car at 10.46. 'Are you ready?' are probably the words I have said to her the most often over the years. When finally she is ready to leave, she has a quick pee, then drinks a glass of water, then has to have another quick pee because of the water she has just drunk. When she is running late and rings someone up to say she will be there in ten minutes, the rest of us snigger and refer to 'Polly minutes', which are between twice and three times as long as a real minute.

My daughter has inherited these genes, rather than mine. She was in the front room with her friend Hedy, deciding what to wear. I went into my room while she was deciding, lay down on the bed to read and, as it was the afternoon and I had enjoyed a copious lunch, woke up forty-five minutes later. They were still in the front room, wearing completely different clothes and no nearer a definitive solution, even though the picnic they were going to had started some time earlier.

Which probably explains why I have traditionally been in a bit of a hurry. But it doesn't explain why I am no longer in a hurry, why there no longer seems a need to be busy-busy-busy, why a slower life seems a more sensible life.

This is another cousin of the urge to retreat, the loss of FOMO, and the loss of ambition. As you gradually excise from your life all the things that you simply cannot be arsed to do, you have so much more time to do other things that you might actually want to do. It is possible, also, that your time-management skills may have improved with age and experience, although obviously we're not counting Polly or my mum. Because you are less busy, you should be more efficient, and you probably get just as much done as you used to because of that increased efficiency. It's a virtuous circle: work less, achieve more. I have written every word so far in this chapter in slightly over an hour, which I couldn't have done twenty years ago. I'll have a bath in a moment, which will help me work out what I am going to say next.

Slowing down, though, is against the spirit of the age. This is a hurly-burly time, where internet speeds are never quite fast enough, where everyone needs a new iPhone yesterday, where the flashing lights and angry voices of social media suck you in like a whirlpool. No one is actually made happier by any of this, of course, which I assume is why everyone in north London has gone for a run, because it's the only way they can escape from the modern world. In my last book, *How to Be a Writer*, I advocated strongly against Twitter, which is an echo chamber for the deranged and almost certainly a force for evil. I hope that by the time this book comes out, people will have finally seen though Twitter, just as I have been hoping for years they would see through plastic surgery, the Conservative Party and Piers Morgan. But it's not going to happen, is it?*

Everyone tells you that you can't resist the speed of modern life, and maybe you can't, but I am having a bloody good go

---

* For many years I thought there couldn't be anyone worse than Piers Morgan, with his big face, vindictive desire for revenge and bulbous sense of entitlement. Then about half a dozen came along at once.

at it. As well as eschewing Twitter, I do not have a mobile phone, and haven't had since September 2016, when I was presenting a quiz in the Long Room at the Oval. I left it on the lectern to go for a pee, and when I returned it had gone. It was only a shabby old £15 Nokia, an abacus in a sea of pocket calculators, already so old-fashioned people looked at it in wonderment. My intention was always to buy another one, sooner or later, and then years began to pass. Initially the problem was one of expense. I already pay out a fortune every month for three mobiles. Did we really need a fourth? At one point this morning Polly's mobile rang and it was our daughter, on her mobile in her bed upstairs, asking for a cup of tea.

As time went on, my reluctance hardened. As one of maybe twelve people in Europe who doesn't have one, I realised that these tiny machines enslave you and twist your very soul around their minuscule electronic requirements. I felt like a bystander in that very scary *Doctor Who* episode (David Tennant era, I think) in which everyone wears metal things in their ears which take them over and turn them into Cybermen. So when I go for a walk, I do so in the sublime and calming knowledge that no one will be able to contact me. No one will know where I am. If I am meeting someone somewhere, I will turn up on time, in the old-fashioned way. 'But suppose you are kidnapped by aliens or killed by a ball of ice-piss* falling from a passing aeroplane?' they cry. In that case, I say, chances are that I won't turn up. They will get over it, although it's possible that I will not.

The ubiquity of mobile phones has changed our landscape and our lives. There are no red phone boxes any more, but

---

* Piss-ice?

as most of them were eventually used only as urinals for the drunk and desperate, I am not sure this is such a bad thing.* Mobiles have made walking up a narrow pavement an act only for the supremely courageous, as you constantly have to swerve to avoid people looking at their phones. Sometimes you see two people approaching from opposite directions while looking at their phones, and for a second or two there's the delicious possibility that they will walk straight into each other and fall over, their legs waving in the air like upturned cockroaches. It hasn't happened yet – some vestigial instinct always manages to kick in at the last moment – but I am relentlessly optimistic and I keep an eye out just in case.

Mobile phones have been bad news for the clock industry. Have you noticed there are no clocks in pubs any more? There are still in barbers, but I'm sure there won't be for long. I don't wear a watch either, mainly because I used to and kept looking at it frantically. If you are not constantly trying to find out what time it is, you develop a curious sixth sense for what time it is. With absolutely no evidence to confirm or deny it, you will know that it's about 3.15 now. Obviously this skill takes a while to develop. When you are young you might think it is 3.15 when it's actually 10.30. But be patient and it will all work out.

'Be patient' could easily have been the title of this chapter. Be patient, slow down, eat a biscuit, stare into space. These are the simple but enormous benefits of getting older, for as your body gets weaker your determination to overcome the

---

* In the countryside many red phone boxes have been repurposed as tiny libraries or homes for defibrillators. Which is why when anyone has a heart attack in a car, the cry immediately goes up of 'Where's the nearest red phone box?'

drivellous distractions of modern life somehow becomes stronger. For some men the rage takes over, and we shall be looking at this later. But for many of us, peace and quiet become the holy grail. When I was young I thought that my elders' yearning for peace and quiet was, frankly, ridiculous. What is actually ridiculous is finding it ridiculous, because peace and quiet are the essence of a good life well lived. They don't really announce their presence, not really being a presence, but more of an absence. But soon they will be your friends and you will welcome their fond embrace. My children say I have a wants-some-peace-and-quiet face, and I wouldn't be surprised if I do. Oddly enough, when everyone else finally goes out and I am left to my own devices, I often put on very loud music and dance pitifully around the flat, but that's just peace and quiet of a surprisingly deafening variety.

Anyway, I interpret the desire for peace and quiet as an entirely natural consequence of ageing, to be welcomed rather than resisted. Your instincts are telling you to take things more slowly, more quietly, and they almost certainly know better than you. Be the age you are, not the age you think you would like to be.

I think this may be the first great paradox of ageing. Trying to stay young, doing all the things you used to do, doing all the things young people now do, puts such a strain on your body and your psyche that it will end up ageing you faster. Whereas if you acknowledge your age and take things more easily, that will actually keep you young.

Think of something you find difficult that you feel you should find easy. The new washing machine, with more lights and buttons than the International Space Station. Or the computer you work with: how do you connect a new printer and make it work in less than a week? Polly spends much of her day shouting at websites. Technology seems designed to confound us, and that's *because it is*. It is not aimed at older people, and there is no shame whatsoever in struggling with it. I'll give you an example. I spent a full year wiggling the lead in my computer every time I wanted to print something out, because it wasn't a good connection and the printer needed to be coaxed into action. Then one day I forgot to plug it in altogether, and Bluetooth kicked in and it printed without the lead in. It had never occurred to me that it could do this. I had registered the word 'Bluetooth' a long time before, but I had simply assumed this was something terribly complicated that I would never be able to understand. I still don't understand it, but I know it works. As for the remote control, this button switches off the Christmas lights over the road and that button launches a telecommunications satellite into outer space.*

It is a common young/oldie gripe that this or that feature of modernity appears to be beyond us. So common, in fact, that we can safely disregard it. My contention is: it doesn't matter. For all of us, our competence has limits, but what we learn as we get older is that our incompetence has no limits at all. So why worry about it? There's nothing you can do about it. Breathe more slowly. Put the kettle on. Be patient. Slow down.

Young people have two valuable roles to play in all this.

---

* It's probably worth repeating here Douglas Adams's three rules that describe our reactions to new technology. '1. Anything that is in the world when you're born is normal and ordinary and is just a natural part of the way the world works. 2. Anything that's invented between when you're fifteen and thirty-five is new and exciting and revolutionary and you can probably get a career in it. 3. Anything invented after you're thirty-five is against the natural order of things.'

One is that they know how to switch on the dishwasher without fusing all the lights in the street, and they can get you out of the feedback loop of hell on the latest badly designed website. The other is that, unwittingly, they show you what not to do. Some youngish people live opposite me, a couple, probably in their mid-thirties. I haven't spoken to them, but they have only been there a couple of years, and we are British, after all. (I stood with them at the pedestrian crossing at the end of the road the other day and we steadfastly ignored each other.) They are very busy people, constantly doing things, going places, taking the rubbish out, doing DIY, driving off, driving back, busy-busy-busy. I am not sure I have ever seen either of them smile.

At least they haven't put a sofa out on the street yet. People are constantly doing that around here, for the council to take away, and maybe for desperate paups to cart away under the night sky. All of these sofas are perfectly serviceable. Maybe a little battered, maybe a little stained, but their only sin, it seems to me, is that they are no longer absolutely brand new, so I presume their owners have got slightly bored with them, bunged them out on the pavement and gone off to Sofas R Us to buy a new one. THIS IS MADNESS.

When we were in our forties and fifties, quite a lot of my friends did up their houses in such a way that you almost thought some adults lived there. Bold wall colours, expensive carpets, new unstained sofa, armchairs they might have inherited from a deceased aunt, bookshelves full of hardbacks, a roaring log fire ... you couldn't help but be impressed, and I was, time and time again, especially when contemplating the ratty old carpets and chipped paint of our own, rather more disgusting flat.

But when you have slowed down, you see no reason to dispose of a slightly battered sofa, you see no need to go shopping for things you don't need, you see no point in going through the enormous effort and expense of redecorating, not just yet. So, fifteen years later, all these once elegantly appointed show houses are looking a bit threadbare. Most of them need a lick of paint, or rather more than a lick. Because my friends all seem to have had the same thought: This'll do. We can't be bothered. What an upheaval it would be, and for what? We'll leave it like this. No one will notice, or if they do, they won't care. It doesn't matter. And they are right: no one will and it really doesn't. Slow down. Eat biscuits. Have a bath. Put the kettle on. Don't you worry about a thing.

11

Parents

We have established over the course of several chapters that it's not really so bad being a young/oldie, that there are compensations for your body falling apart and weird little purple veins suddenly appearing on your legs for no apparent reason. But the good news stops here. For now we must deal with an even more depressing subject than your own precipitate decline, and that's the even swifter decline of your ailing, non-functioning, possibly increasingly gaga parents.

I know quite a few people who lost one or both parents young, and I know it's a hole that can never be filled. Parents drive us mad, they have us tearing our hair out in frustration, but unless they have been spectacularly useless, we want them to live long and healthy lives and to keep annoying us into sprightly old age. (You will know when you yourself become truly old, because people will start describing you as 'sprightly'.) In fact, parents are so crucial that many people love them even when they *have* been spectacularly useless. There would be no psychotherapists if that last sentence were not true. They would all be working in Tesco and thinking their deep thoughts to no purpose at all.

But if your parents have survived, there's their old age to deal with, and the person who will be dealing with it will probably be you and your siblings (if any). At our WALLS meetings, we first describe our aches and pains, then discuss our latest medications, and then move on to our parents. Of the six of us, one has no parents left, I am the only one with two, and the rest all have one each. Of those, one lives in Australia, which is a very long way away indeed, and the other three are all in old age's endgame: two with dementia and the third bedridden for physical ailments. The group has also lost three parents over the past two years. All of them lived to a great age, though one or two thought that Sir Alec Douglas-Home was still prime minister.*

If Alzheimer's (which we shall use as shorthand for a smorgasbord of age-related dementias) was contagious, it would be the new pandemic. Many more people appear to have it than they used to, because many more people are living to a great age. When I was young my great-grandmother lived to ninety-seven, and my mother had a great-aunt who made it to 101. Both were considered extraordinary. Now it's almost routine. The youngest WALLS parent is eighty-six and most are well into their nineties. So prevalent has Alzheimer's become that when your parents don't have it, it seems like a miracle. You actively rejoice, although very quietly, because your friends with gaga parents wouldn't appreciate it. But the worry never entirely recedes. Even if your parent can still

---

* While this book was being written, two more died, although I still (unfashionably) have both of mine.

stride up a mountain and recite all their times tables without a pause for breath, you never stop looking for signs of mental decline. Because if the aged one does fall prey, you know it won't just be their life that turns to shit: it will be yours too.

I have one friend whose mother is old, fragile and living alone, and he also has responsibility for an elderly aunt and uncle. He goes and sees his mother twice a week, and his aunt and uncle once a fortnight, which isn't a lot, but it feels like more, he says, because he is so exhausted afterwards, from worry and sadness, he cannot function properly for hours.

Another friend's father, eighty-nine, is still in his home and being looked after by carers. But he's reached the stage of dementia at which he keeps pooing on the sofa, so my friend has suggested to his two younger brothers that he be moved into a care home. But the brothers are from a different mother. My friend's mother died many years ago and left him her house, so the agreement was that their father would leave his money to the two younger boys (men now in their fifties). Payment for a care home would come out of their legacy. They don't like this. Indeed, since my friend made his suggestion, they have stopped speaking to him. My friend, who used to go and see his father once a week, hasn't been able to see him for six months. 'Would he have noticed?' I asked him. 'No, he hasn't a clue who I am,' he said, 'but that's not the point.'

A third has a mother who has had dementia for seven or eight years. 'All through the Covid pandemic, I just hoped that she would catch it and quietly die,' he admitted to me recently, after he had had a few. 'But no such luck.'

For a while I wondered why some people with Alzheimer's die quite quickly and others go on for years. It's to do with which part of the brain the disease affects, which appears to be random. If it gets you in a part of the brain which is vital for continued existence, it's goodnight Vienna. But if it attacks a less crucial part of the brain – say, the part that knows that Jeremy Vine and Jeremy Paxman are two different people – you can go on indefinitely.

Personally, I think the first option is much the better one. If I ever get it, I'd like to be dead by a week next Tuesday.

The sons and daughters of people with Alzheimer's often seem to agree.

Although they might not say so in so many words.

To anyone other than themselves.

Alzheimer's may not be contagious, but there is a genetic component. Which means that if it is in your family, you are more likely to get it yourself sooner or later, and if one of your parents suffers from it, you are even more likely.

So that's fun, isn't it. Not only do you have to look after this dribbling incontinent husk of a person you have loved all your life, but at the back of your mind lurks the thought that one day this may well happen to you as well. Something else to wake you at five in the morning, bathed in sweat and silently screaming.

Every time I see Jeremy Vine on the television, I say to Polly, if I ever think that's Jeremy Paxman, drop everything, call Dignitas and book me a one-way ticket to Switzerland. But Polly is not listening. She is doing the quick crossword in the paper and can't remember the word for 'tractor'. It's the first sign, she mumbles almost inaudibly, the first sign . . .

'Parents' is the first chapter title so far that I have reused from *A Shed of One's Own*, but re-reading that chapter just now I was surprised to see that it was mainly about being a parent of small children, and not as much about our own parents. But my children are now big and my focus has changed. I tend to phone my mother every other day, and she rings for a chat about as often. This didn't happen ten years ago, but she wasn't ninety-one ten years ago. Many of us are now much kinder and more accepting of our parents, as we are of our friends, because every interaction with them is underpinned by the knowledge that time is limited. If we lived for ever, would this happen? Would a 150-year-old me have mellowed towards his 179-year-old mother, or would he find her as fantastically irritating as he did when he was younger? It's the limit of life that gives it its flavour, and only now our own and our parents' lives are clearly limited do we really begin to understand that.

The chapter on parents in *Shed* ended with a rather good paragraph, which I shall quote here in full, because it still applies.

Some people say you don't really become a grown-up until your parents have died. I have always hated that idea, which seems small consolation for the fact that your parents have died. And what is a grown-up, anyway? Is it such a good thing to be that it is worth paying such a hefty price? Find me anyone who says yes and I'll show you either a liar or a pompous, emotionally cauterised middle-aged man whose inner child is lonely and crying and as lost as anyone can be.

Which tells me, among other things, that I was terrified of my mother dying ten years ago, just as I am terrified of it today. And absurdly grateful that it hasn't happened yet.

Of course all this depends on the quality of the parenting you yourself received, and in Britain the upper and upper-middle classes have this strange habit of sending their children away to boarding school at the age of seven. They grow into the pompous, emotionally cauterised men of whom I wrote, a fair few of whom become prime minister. So the job that most needs empathy and understanding of the way people live more often than not goes to a shallow, self-centred posh man who only wants the job because he hopes it will make him feel nice. And we wonder why we are a nation in decline.

Nonetheless, if your parenting was good enough and at least one of your parents is still alive, the young/old years do present an opportunity to get close to them in a new and different way. It's not quite a relationship of equals – I am not sure it ever can be – but what might now be equal, if you are lucky, is the love and affection you feel for each other. As a small child you were utterly dependent on your parents; as a teenager and young adult you sloughed off this skin and emerged like a slightly spotty butterfly. Only in the later years, and possibly after you have had children, do you understand life from their angle, and I think the love simply evens up. They need and love you for the same reason they have always needed and loved you, because they are your parents and no love in the world exceeds parental love. You need and love them because you have come to appreciate and value them more, and possibly because they can't tell you what to do any more. Not that that stops them having a go, but it's an old habit, easily disregarded.*

---

* When I was growing up, my mother, whenever she was going out and leaving me alone, would always say, 'Don't answer the door to anyone.' I reminded her of this the other day, and added that the last time she said this to me, I was over thirty.

The poorly parented, by contrast, are probably still grappling with their demons, for this has become a lifetime's quest. It's mellow and mad all over again. The void at their core can never be adequately filled. It's that important. Which may be another reason why we start to feel more grateful to our parents as we get older, because if we are at all functional it is pretty much all down to them. We may have made what we can of our lives with the raw materials we were given, but if we were given no raw materials we can make nothing. A bad workman blames his tools, or his parents if he has no tools.

12

Children

It seems absurdly simplistic to say this, but by the age of sixty you will either have children or you will not. It's strikingly unlikely, in other words, that this will change, that if you haven't any children yet, you might have one or two at some point in the future. It could happen, in much the same way that Exeter City could play Cambridge United in the final of the European Champions League. And if it does happen, as previously stated, it will age you like a magical ageing drug, possibly the most effective such drug yet developed.

I think it's fair to say, though, that at sixty, if you haven't had kids, you are living a different life to those of us who have. You are much richer, for one thing. You probably look about ten years younger and it's possible that, from time to time, you might actually be having some sex with someone. But as one childless friend of mine regularly moans, who is going to look after me when I am old? Actually, the couples with children say the same thing, because their children have already made it clear that they have other fish to fry.

It's not about that, though. It's about love. Unless you are damaged beyond measure, the love you feel for your children exceeds all other forms of love. It feels like a love of a different order of magnitude. And while you may no longer love, or even like, your partner in life, you do share with them one unique characteristic: you are the only two people in the world who love your children as much as you do. You are the only two people in the world who *can* love your children as much as you do. It's this knowledge, alone, that keeps millions of long-dead marriages going. (That and the cost of divorce, which is prohibitive.)

When my kids were small I wrote a book called *Fatherhood: The Truth*, which purported to take you through the early years of this process in as painless a way as possible, starting at conception and ending at the first birthday party.* In it I described how having children changes you, and I think the analogy still holds true. Imagine a vista in front of you, about the size and shape of a wide-screen television. This represents your life before children, and it's very full. Work, hobbies, socialising, family, love, sex, alcohol, cold takeaway pizza for breakfast: how could we possibly fit babies into all that? Then the babies arrive and the vista simply expands to accommodate them. The vista, it turns out, is mutable, and so are you. It's true that the children will gradually push out things you will no longer have time for, but you don't mind, even though you complain incessantly about sleep deprivation, changing nappies, the cost of everything and your

---

* Some years later I came up with the idea for a sequel, to be entitled *Fatherhood: The Fish Finger Years*. Then I discovered that someone else had already written a book called *The Fish Finger Years*, and with the title gone, the whole idea for the book simply vanished from my mind, as though it had never been.

terrible back problems as the children get bigger but still want to be picked up. And when this early, frontline phase has come to an end, when the children have grown enough to realise that you talk complete rubbish quite a lot of the time, you will remember how exhausted and bad-tempered you always were, and you will miss it. You will look at younger parents starting out on the same route, with their pasty skin and eyes that look as though they have been punched repeatedly, and you won't envy them ... except that you will, a bit.

Of course, with love comes vulnerability. You are beholden to your children in ways that they really don't want to know about. You want everything to be all right for them. You want them to flourish and find their role in adult life. You would rather they didn't smoke or take hard drugs or drive like lunatics. But at the same time, you probably want them to be themselves and not your version of themselves, or anybody else's, come to that.

My daughter, aged twenty-three, likes talking about this, usually while cleaning out the fridge as though she hasn't eaten for two weeks (and putting on no weight at all afterwards). She can already see friends of hers who had stern, controlling fathers going for a similar type of man in their early romantic lives, and knows there's no point at all telling them this, if she wants them to remain her friends. She has an emotional intelligence it took me several more decades to gain. She is blissfully, often furiously herself.

My son, aged twenty, expresses himself most articulately in sport. Although he has never knowingly read a book, he is blond, ridiculously tall, handsome, full of genuine charm, kind and gentle. He will go far. They both will. I am pathetically proud of them both.

Every parent you will talk to will say similar things, even if their child has serious problems, even if their child is a registered basket case. At WALLS, four out of six of us have children, and we all dote on them. Worse, we boast about them, which is lovely for us but boring for everyone else. Never ask a proud father how his children are, because he will tell you, until physically restrained.

Some of my friends who mellowed rather than went mad did so really because of their children. It's hard to remain an alpha male, ripping up trees with your bare hands, after you have carried your baby in a sling for a while. I would recommend hands-on parenthood as a cure for almost all psychological ailments. The realisation that it isn't all about you is actually life-affirming. Narcissists and psychopaths will never feel this, of course, because life truly is only about them. But then very rarely are they hands-on parents. My father certainly wasn't, for he was of a generation that believed looking after children was women's work. I doubt he ever changed my nappy. He also expressed the view that women should not be allowed to own property by law, but that's another issue.

But with vulnerability comes fear. I don't know a single parent who isn't terrified that their child will die before them. I think it might be the worst thing that can possibly happen to you. Your own life? You'd give that up in a microsecond if it would save your child.[*]

I have known people whose child was stillborn and is still

---

[*] When the singer-songwriter Kirsty MacColl was killed by a speedboat in the Gulf of Mexico in 2000, she was pushing her then fifteen-year-old son Jamie out of its path. People who don't understand why she did this either do not have children of their own or are very much not be trusted.

mourned. One couple always say they have three daughters, although only two are still alive. Another couple's stillborn son would have been their fifth child, and it's more than twenty years ago, but each year on his birthday the whole family go to his grave and cry their eyes out.

I have known another couple whose daughter died at two years and ten months. She was a sprite, never destined for a long life: she had a rare medical condition and her parents knew she could die at any time. My daughter, then aged two years and four months, went up to say goodnight to her, and came down and said she was worried about her. The little girl died in the night. At the funeral, little boxes of Smarties (her favourite) were left on every seat. I managed to eat all of mine before I started blubbing.

Casualties were suspiciously high at my school. One boy, called Reddington, had a hole in the heart: he was eleven or twelve when he died. A boy called Greenhalgh died of a mysterious tropical disease during the summer holidays. A boy called Taggart lost his leg to bone cancer at about fourteen, and didn't last very long after that. A boy called Freddie Purbeck, a year above me, jumped out of a window after his mother died. Rob Zikel, our head of house, died aged twenty of leukaemia. This was the 1970s: cancers were usually fatal. And countless boys died in car accidents not wearing seatbelts.

At university a young journalist I knew called Philip Geddes was in Harrods doing some Christmas shopping when he heard something was going on outside the store. He went to investigate and as he arrived the car bomb exploded. He died instantly.

One of my best friends was an exceptionally talented

physicist called Brian Warr, who after his starred first went to Caltech to begin his academic career. He died of some unspecified cancer aged thirty-one. My friend Matthew did a bit of digging and discovered that not only was Brian gay – which he had never told us, even though it was blindingly obvious in hindsight – but that he had died of Aids. This was 1992, when people still called it the 'gay plague', a very slightly loaded phrase that makes me want to vomit even as I type it.

Another of my best friends at university, Esther Kaposi, died aged forty-four of a brain tumour. She was survived not only by her parents, but by two grandparents, who had both made it out of Auschwitz.

My schoolfriend and long-time collaborator Harry Thompson died aged forty-five of lung cancer, never having smoked a cigarette. His father, whose only child Harry was, survived him, as he had previously survived both his wives. (He died in a house fire in his mid-eighties.)

My dear friend K lost her only son when he was nineteen. F was depressed, like so many nineteen-year-olds, and committed suicide. But at nineteen we have no idea, not even the glimmering of an idea, what our continued existence means to others. K's health, never robust, went into a precipitous decline thereafter, from which it never recovered.* And F's old friends from school were so shocked by the event that, as one of them said to me at the funeral, 'F will never know it, but he will save quite a few lives. People who might have killed themselves now won't.'

All of these people, when they died, left parents, and in Esther's case, grandparents.

---

* She died in April 2023.

You may wonder how I have known so many people who have died. I have been wondering for years. My partner knew no one who had died, literally no one, until her grandmother went when she was in her mid-forties. Whereas people seem to have been keeling over all my life. I have come to the conclusion that I am some kind of Typhoid Mary: perfectly healthy and functional in myself, but lethal to passers-by. To know me is to love me, obviously, but to know me is also to croak, prematurely.

I think it's best if we really don't know what our children are up to. My daughter told me recently about a holiday to Greece she had undertaken with her friend Hedy when they were both seventeen. The ridiculous risks they took would turn your hair white overnight, and I could feel my testicles contracting as she spoke. I won't go into details, but they could have been killed a dozen times in ways even our most violent crime writers haven't yet thought of. To hear about it five years later is far better than hearing about it at the time, and nearly as good as not hearing about it at all.

Youth is a cavalcade of near misses. Young/oldies are instinctively more cautious, although they are in danger themselves far less often. If your young person is unlucky and does die, you will blame yourself for ever, because how can you not? But the alternative is to keep them under wraps for ever, mollycoddled functions of your own fear. Then you gradually turn into one of those stern, controlling fathers, who are never any good for anyone. You will make yourself unhappy and your children unhappy. That's not much of a score. Far better to let them go and fuck up in their own inimitable way. And cross your fingers that they come back unscathed.

As we now know, life is full of risks. The illusion so many of us suffer from is that we can control many of these risks through sheer willpower. I would suggest it is literally insane to believe this. Shit happens, but occasionally, as my daughter and Hedy found in Greece, shit does not happen. For the young, exploring these possibilities is one of the joys of life. Is this nice hairy Greek man really offering me a lift to my hotel, or is he going to lock me in his basement dungeon and use me as a sex toy for twenty-seven years? Toss a coin. Heads or tails?

You have to be swift on your feet to be a parent these days. Everything is changing so fast, and this is happening at precisely the moment in our lives when we are not really geared up for fast changes, or any change at all, if we are to be honest. For instance, although I drink like a fish, I have never taken any form of illegal drug, as I may have mentioned earlier. But both of my kids had smoked weed by mid-adolescence, and most of their friends seem now to be drug hoovers of epic, Keith Richards-like range and proportions. 'If it's a pill, he'll take it,' says my daughter of one of her university friends, with slight disapproval. When she was ten she went out one day and got her ears pierced. I was horrified when she returned, but that lasted about twenty minutes before I had stopped noticing her tiny metal earblobs and it was only about another six months before I stopped addressing her as 'gypsy girl'. She says she would like to have a small tattoo one day, and I have said, as long as it's only small, and she looks at me with the withering disdain all daughters have for their hopeless fuddy-duddy fathers. Her ears are rapidly filling up with metal: one or two of her piercings apparently channel

Netflix direct to her visual cortex. She is a young woman in a hurry, and never more pressed for time than when she rings me up to ask for money.

All these changes – tattoos, piercings, widespread avail-ability of drugs – seem to have happened very quickly, and the latest issue to contend with is the whole trans business. If one of my children said they wanted to change sex, I would be surprised, because he is tall and big-boned, and she is small and fragile. But I have an old friend whose twenty-five-year-old son is in the process of becoming his daughter, whose partner is a woman transforming into a man. Hormones work, but only very slowly, and neither of them have been taking them for long enough to show any substantive difference. But my friend has trained himself to use the correct pronouns and not to use their deadnames, because it's his child and he's on her side, because you can't not be, whatever the fuck they get up to. Unless you are driven by the power of your religious convictions that what they are doing is fundamentally wrong, in which case you will probably never see them again, and the loss will be yours.

There's a far greater horror, though, than your child taking too many drugs, or getting a sleeve tattoo all the way down one arm, or getting so many piercings they jangle when they walk, or becoming a transgender sex worker in the shrub-beries of London's Royal Parks, and that's when they move abroad. I have one friend whose three daughters have moved to the East End of London (acceptable), Amsterdam (on the verge of acceptable) and Melbourne (entirely unacceptable in my opinion). I have another friend whose middle daughter got married to an American and moved to California, where they have had a baby. This friend is in long-term mourning for their absence from his life, but he is bearing up, and the good news is that the American husband has told his wife that he hates it over there now and would like to move back to the UK sooner rather than later. My friend told me this with an unaccustomed spring in his step, looking roughly fifteen years younger than he has done recently – i.e. he now looks roughly the same age he is in real life.*

Our children grow up (we hope), move out, meet someone, settle down. Many of us would probably call this the best-case scenario, although, obviously, there are other options. If your children start procreating you are suddenly transformed into a grandparent. I have three friends, rough contemporaries, who have attained this noble status, all in the past year or so. They all love it as well, for as every grandparent will tell you, sooner or later you can just give them back. It has all the pleasure of parenthood without all the responsibilities, the grinding poverty, the sleep deprivation or the constant crushing exhaustion. No need to change nappies, either, and if you later spoil them rotten with presents, money and sundry 'treats', that's your choice and no obligation at all. My mother was constantly sending the odd twenty-pound note to my daughter at university, and when we all go out for lunch, she always pays half, knowing the battering my poor debit card takes on a daily basis. But she is ninety-one, it's her money and she can do what she likes with it. If that includes paying for us to have our hall repainted (which I could never have afforded), who am I to argue?

All my new grandparent chums are thrilled to bits with

---

* They have since moved back, to within a few miles of where my friend now lives. Result!

these new babies, who often resemble them in ways that eluded the intervening generation, the one that actually gave birth to the wee things. My daughter looks like both her parents, but in terms of personality she identifies very strongly with her two grandmothers, both of whom she understands at almost a cellular level. I like this a lot. If grandparents are available and willing, they must be made use of, for practical reasons and also for deep emotional reasons. Fortunately, the new grandparents all understand this instinctively. Of course they do. How could it be any other way?

My father was about the same age as I am now when his first grandchildren came along. But he made it clear that he had no interest at all in them: as he told my brother, being a grandfather was 'ageing'. Maybe he was worried it would cramp his style with all the luscious young lovelies he was then squiring. Not that they would have already been put off by his bald bonce, excessive drinking or unpleasant bullying personality, because he had loads of MONEY and that was all that mattered. But I'm still quite impressed that anyone like my old man could find such a magnificently and malignantly narcissistic justification for not even acknowledging the existence of the next generation of Berkmanns. My brother, in a display of touching but utterly misplaced loyalty, actually named his second child after the old monster. One year, on the little boy's birthday, my brother texted my father to let him know. Instantly came back a reply: 'I don't give a flying fuck if it's your son's birthday'. I don't think my brother ever reminded him again.

13

Invisible

Middle-aged women often complain that they have become invisible, mainly to men of a similar age who only look at younger women. They are right. Obviously men in their fifties and sixties are not hugely interested in women of the same age, because these men still regard themselves as about forty on a good day, even if those good days come round less and less frequently. But what the women of a certain age may not realise is that the younger women are not actually looking back at the older men, because they too have become invisible. Even if we have kept in reasonable shape – which terrifyingly few of us have done – these younger women are simply no longer interested in us. You can chat to them, baby, flirt a little maybe, but does her mother know that she's out? And when Björn Ulvaeus wrote those lyrics he was thirty-three, and obviously feeling his age as he cruised the grimy nightspots of Stockholm in search of totty. At sixty-two, if you're really lucky they'll let you buy them dinner. But that's all you're getting. We have joined the vast ranks of the unseen. We're like zombies, only we're still breathing.

The invisibility factor applies equally to those of us in long-term relationships as well as those who are not. A quick straw poll of my friends and contemporaries confirms my assumption that none of us are getting any sex at all, either with our wives or with anyone else. The only ones who are getting any are those previously chucked out by their wives for some poor behaviour, who now find themselves in a new relationship with a younger woman. Their gratitude is obviously unbounded, as mine would be if something similar ever happened to me. This woman actually wants to sleep with me? Is she entirely sure about that? The maximum negotiable age gap appears to be about twenty years, so at sixty we might still be attractive to women in their early forties, especially those with poor eyesight. Fifty-year-old women will take a man of seventy, and sixty-year-olds will go up to eighty, although there she might start to think of herself less as a lover than a live-in carer. I know a woman who started going out with her husband when she was twenty-five and he was a young buck of no more than fifty. She is now in her sixties and he has just turned ninety. She says she still loves him, but I doubt that their house is a hotbed of carnal excess. Unless she is knocking off her personal trainer, and to be honest I wouldn't blame her if she was.

Remember that it is one thing to fancy the young, free and single; it is entirely another to be fancied back. They may find your money captivating, if you have any, and they may be impressed by your worldly air, your immeasurable experience of life and those distinguished-looking alcoholic red patches on your cheeks. But no young woman has ever said the words 'I love all that hair growing out of your ears' or 'How do you get your eyebrows so bushy?' Unfortunately, although our bodies may be sixty and above, our minds are about seventeen. We are the new incels (involuntary celibates), a term previously applied only to the young men who become radicalised misogynists because girls of the same age won't give them the time of day. Don't blame the girls, who are all eyeing up men of a few years older, or at least the ones who haven't grown appalling beards. But they are not eyeing up you and me, which is our tragedy, unless we are hugely rich and/or narcissistic alpha males. When I was young, I used to hate the older men who had their pick of the younger women I knew. I still do, although their equivalents now are years and years younger than me. Eventually, as my mother has confirmed, absolutely everyone is younger than you. Everyone left, that is. And by then, you're more invisible than you could ever imagine.

Unfortunately, it is in the nature of some men – and I am one of them – to suffer enormous crushes on women who are entirely unattainable: either they are four hundred years younger than you, or they have a boyfriend who represents his country at taekwondo. It seems to be getting worse as I get older, not better, and as it gets worse the chance you can do something about it recedes into the distance, like your health and your hair. I occasionally get looks from older women, often in their sixties or seventies, whose husbands may have died, or walled themselves up in their sheds, but who still have some snap in their celery. These looks often have an undercurrent of visits to National Trust properties and their attendant tea-rooms, where knees could possibly be fondled. As you can see, I may not have an actual sex life, but I have an unusually rich imaginative sex life, as do many of my male friends. It's a consolation, if a very, very small one.

Several female friends have reported fallings-off of their

libidos, with one or two expressing deep satisfaction that they are 'past all that now'. God, if only. Actually, I would miss it if it were gone, as it dominates my life to an unhealthy extent. I am someone who can fall in love three times walking up to the off-licence, and three more times walking home again. It's exhausting but not unenjoyable.

I have often wondered about libido: how much is in the mind and how much is in the sweaty groin area? How much is a relationship about sex anyway? Given how many couples I know stopped doing it years ago, I would say very little. Few couples seem to stay together for the sex, and those who do (and seem to talk about it endlessly) are just annoying. Instead, people talk self-importantly about 'companionship', which for all but the very rich translates into a strong desire not to live in a bedsit eating Pot Noodles and masturbating furiously to the internet. Maybe the companionship of some-one you have known intimately for years and who wishes you dead only from time to time, but you know would never have the energy to kill you, is better than nothing, which is the only viable alternative.

The main priority for the late-middle-aged man is not to be a perv, or a predator. Which I really am not, so it's no effort at all, although it's probably just as important not to be seen as a perv or a predator.* I have known a few men who were genuine predators, and some who were actually proud of it. Such men often think they need women, and they certainly

---

* In 2020 the Hollywood actor Dennis Quaid married a woman thirty-nine years younger than him. Someone on Twitter did the sums. 'His first wife was three years older than he was. His second wife (Meg Ryan) was ten years younger. His third wife was twenty years younger. His fourth wife will be forty years younger. Dennis Quaid's fifth wife hasn't been born yet.'

want women, but do they actually like women? Each one was profoundly misogynist in his core, and all have generated chaos and destruction in the lives of the women they pursued and caught. Some women are repeatedly attracted to men who behave like this. I have one friend, whom we shall call N, who had a fiftieth birthday party, a joint one with her husband of the time, and invited fifty guests, of whom forty-nine were her friends and just one was his, who was his secretary. The marriage didn't last long after that. He was a rich and successful barrister, who turned out to be knobbing the secretary, and was sacked from his chambers for so doing. He then divorced my friend N and claimed poverty because he was unemployed and she had owned the house that they had lived in, a house she had to sell to pay him the substantial sum of money a foolish judge decided she owed him. Shortly afterwards he got some enormously well-paid job elsewhere and no doubt continues to wreak havoc with people's lives to this day. N had been out with men like this before and has been out with someone similar since. She recognises that this is an addiction she desperately has to kick if she is to find true happiness with someone who isn't actually a nutter and has no friends because he can't trust anyone and therefore can't be trusted himself. One of her previous boyfriends was known to me. He remains one of two men I know at whose weddings there was no best man, because neither of them trusted anyone enough to give the sort of speech they wanted, rather than actually deserved.

So if that's the choice – be an alpha-male predator or become invisible – I shall happily take invisibility. Of course you could always chase one of those invisible middle-aged women. There are enough of them around. But would they notice? Would anyone?

14

Facelift

Things move apace in the exciting, go-ahead world of plastic surgery. Where once, not so long ago, it was only the rich and daft choosing to have cosmetic surgery, now everybody's doing it. Walk down any London street at almost any time of day and you will see a woman who's had her lips done, or had a nose job, or had a boob job, or had that strangest and most mysterious of all procedures, a Brazilian butt lift. This didn't even exist a decade ago, and now it's the fastest-growing plastic surgery item on the menu. It essentially consists of removing fat from where you don't want it – let's say, your huge belly gutbag – and depositing it on your bottom, giving you a bum like Kim Kardashian's and probably making getting in and out of the bath very difficult indeed. The upside is that if you lean forward you have essentially given yourself a new shelf on your body, and if there's one thing certain in life it's that we all need more storage space. The downside is that your body becomes so unbalanced that you probably fall over all the time. The only solution to this problem is to have enormous fake boobs installed, to keep you upright for minutes at a go.

The other downside, possibly more serious, is that having a Brazilian butt lift is not an uncomplicated procedure, and people have a tendency to die on the operating table. Which seems a bit drastic when all you had to do was eat several pizzas a day and then exercise vigorously to direct all your lovely new fat to your arse cheeks. (If that's possible, of course.) But surgery, although riskier, is a quicker solution to your lack of an enormous pair of buttocks.

I don't actually know any women who have had a bum-related procedure, but I know loads who have had a nip here, a tuck there. Not that we have discussed it, because we're English, and they would ascribe their suddenly healthier, younger look to their new vegan diet, moisturiser and buckets of herbal tea. I know a couple of women, both in their sixties, who now look ridiculously young, one because she apparently has a secret lover, whom everyone seems to know about so he's not quite as secret as she thinks he is, and the other one who seems very happy with her seventy-year-old crock of a husband, and he seems pretty happy with her too – unless she also has a younger lover she feels she has to keep up with. I don't know; I merely speculate. Come to think of it, speculating might be more fun than knowing for certain.

The other two big risers on the plastic surgery charts are lip fillers and Botox. We have all seen the results of lip fillers on reality shows such as *Love Island* and *The Only Way Is Essex*, where young women barely out of their teens are having the placentas of recently pregnant sheep (or some such) injected into their lips to give them a permanently plumped, ready-for-oral-sex look. Fine, if that's the impression you want to give while buying a packet of loo roll in Sainsbury's, but when you trawl through Instagram, as everyone now does on public transport, you notice that all these young women look exactly the same: beautiful in an artificial, manufactured way, like little Stepford Wives on a production line, ready to be married off to narcissistic alpha males who will treat them atrociously, and then dump them when their enormous lips and buttocks go out of fashion, as they will one day. There's got to be more to life than this, surely?

Quite a few women of my acquaintance seem to have embraced Botox and other non-surgical methods of staying young. Botox is, of course, a deadly poison if consumed in high enough quantities, and if I were given the chance to have regular injections of arsenic, strychnine or polonium-210 in my face to ease out a few of my increasingly canyon-like wrinkles, I would choose to remain the old wreck I am. Regular users of Botox lose the ability to form facial expressions at all, which I would have thought would not be helpful to actors and actresses of a certain age, for whom forming facial expressions is one of their core skills. After a few Botox injections (and indeed, after proper plastic surgery), your skin starts to look buffed and slightly shiny, and you begin to resemble a full-sized *Thunderbirds* puppet. Simon Cowell, who once said that 'to me, Botox is no more unusual than toothpaste', now looks remarkably like Virgil Tracy, and has married a woman young enough to be his wife, if you see what I mean. His teeth are so white you can't help wondering whose they were before he had them installed.

My opinion of all these horror-measures, which make you look like a gruesomely reordered parody of yourself, has not changed since I wrote about them in *Shed*:

All this stuff seems to say something terrible about life as it is now lived. If we feel so impelled to amend ourselves in these violent ways, it suggests that we never much liked what we were. That's hardly surprising: the underlying message of most advertising and the entire fashion industry is that we are not much cop, and really need to shape up. To be alive in the early twenty-first century is to be made to feel that you are not quite good enough. What's so sad is that by the time middle age creeps along, you would hope you would finally feel comfortable in your own skin. I'm not sure anyone could feel truly comfortable in something so stretched ...

I would like to think that, sometime in the future, it will gradually dawn on us all that to undergo unnecessary cosmetic surgery is to broadcast your unhappiness to the world, that it is a cry for help, and a long, keening wail at that. In 2007 the novelist Olivia Goldsmith, who wrote *The First Wives Club*, fell into a coma and died in New York after undergoing what one paper euphemistically called 'elective facial surgery'. What a grim and pointless way to go. Worse, it's a death that makes your whole life look ridiculous. It's like those men who die in hotel rooms in weird auto-erotic asphyxiation incidents, with satsumas in their mouths and chair legs up their bottoms. Everything they achieved in their lives is deleted by this single absurd act, which speaks to the rest of us only of unfathomable misery.

No famous person has yet croaked on the operating table while having a Brazilian butt lift, but it will happen before long. I wonder, is it just a one-off operation or do you have to take it in to be serviced, like an old car? How nice it is to get honestly old and realise that you are never going to have to worry about such things.

And yet, how can we be absolutely sure that friends of ours, whether male or female, have not had some 'elective facial surgery' to freshen their spring look? I have a feeling that men will start travelling down this dangerous road more and more often. Soon it won't just be Silvio Berlusconi who looks as though someone has polished his face with Mr Sheen. Donald Trump may have been the first bald US president since Gerald Ford, but his successor Joe Biden may be the first US president of all time to have had an obvious hair transplant. Some observers believe he has also had his wrinkles done and porcelain veneers stuck on his teeth. If this is all true, he could lay claim to being the first bionic president. Where politicians (and Simon Cowell) venture, the rest of us eventually follow. Will my more corpulent male friends start having liposuction to dispose of their huge stomachs? Or have laser treatment on their revolting hairy backs? Sting used to say that cocaine was God's way of telling you you had too much money, but I think plastic surgery may have superseded that. It rests in the demilitarised zone between dignity and vanity, where some of the most brutal wars on the planet continue to wage. It's all too revolting even to contemplate, so I suggest we move on as swiftly as our still elegant Fred Astaire legs can carry us.

15

Vanity

... thy name is Marcus, or David, or Roger, or Neil. As discussed before, men look in the mirror and think, Yeah, that'll do, when it manifestly won't. Whereas women, looking in the mirror, are more likely to be hyper-critical of their looks and will therefore expend limitless time and energy making things look very slightly better. This is why women are almost always at least presentable at the age of sixty and men, bluntly, are not. But we accuse women of being vain because of their capacity for self-improvement, whereas I think it's the men who are vain because they see only perfection where there isn't any. Vanity here is a close relative of complacency. A good example of this is the author photograph on books such as this one. My own author photograph was taken in 2005. I had it professionally done, and it cost me £200. I have been too skint and lazy to get another one done that admits to the physical decline of the past few years, but there's another consideration, which is that the 2005 photograph represents the way I continue to see myself in my mind's eye. Which turns out to need glasses even though my real eyes do not.

Have I genuinely been too skint and lazy to get another photo done? Even as I type the words it sounds like an excuse to me, because the intervening years have not been especially kind:

Me in 2005

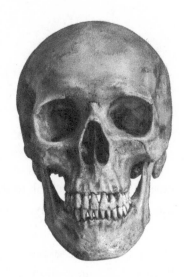

Now

Some of my friends look even worse.

To be precise, I think that male vanity works together with anti-vanity, although you have to be careful with such combustible substances: should a particle of vanity coincide with a similar particle of anti-vanity, there would be a giant rip in the space-time continuum which might mean the end of all life in the universe. Anti-vanity manifests itself not only in the disastrous facial hair of the young (and also of the old-but-should-know-better) but in the clothes choices we all make day to day. Many men believe that they look fine in anything they wear; indeed, that they are wearing it makes it, de facto, acceptable. So many of them will wear pretty much anything: disastrous knitwear, bedraggled fleeces, tank tops, suits. I believe that many men wear a suit and tie because it absolves them from the need to make any sort of real decision, let alone an actual choice. The polka dot tie or the paisley tie? Does it matter? Not even slightly. The insouciance with which some men wear awful cricket- or golf-club ties slightly takes the breath away.

But it's in leisurewear that many men truly come a cropper. As spring edges tentatively into summer, many of them who live round here adopt the classic summer ensemble of daggy old T-shirt, disgraceful shorts, white socks and scabby old trainers, whether it's warm enough to bare your knees to the elements or whether it's not. On occasion the socks are pulled up high and become a pair of scoutmaster's socks, which by rights would be subject to prosecution and eventual detention at His Majesty's Pleasure. I'm not sure what's worse: scabby old trainers that appear to have already run around the world, possibly both ways, or 'box-fresh' new trainers costing about as much as a small car. Neither are appropriate. The daggy old T-shirt usually advertises some terrible old band that split up in 1986, or maybe it was their ill-fated reunion tour of 2009. And what's wrong with shorts that go below the knee, thus protecting the public from the need to see the knobbly knees in all their glory? In high summer all the local pubs become informal festivals of body hair. Some men have so much it almost qualifies as an extra organ. If they shaved it off they would probably lose half a stone. Other men, weirdly, don't seem to have any at all. Has it all fallen out? Did they never have any? Do they shave it off to augment their aerodynamic qualities when riding their sad middle-aged bicycles?* I saw a fat man with no leg hair in the pub the other day. He had no aerodynamic qualities to speak of. I doubt he'd been on a bike in thirty years. If he could fly he would be an airship.

I don't want to have these thoughts, but the men of my neighbourhood, with their hideous bodies and ill-considered clothing, have forced them into my head.

What women learn is what suits them and what doesn't. You wouldn't wear a short skirt if you had fat thighs and massive calves. So why do so many men wear shorts? I don't believe that anyone should wear a T-shirt after the age of about twenty-eight. Especially when (like me) you have weedy upper arms, or (unlike me) you have a huge fat stomach. And very especially when you have enough body hair to stuff a sofa.

Formal male clothing, by contrast, has an elegance that does not rely on body shape for its effects. Fat, thin, tall, fun-sized, it doesn't matter what you look like with your clothes off, because as soon as you put on a dinner jacket with black tie or a morning coat (for a wedding) you look the business. It's another reason why men wear suits a lot, because almost no one looks bad in a suit, unless you have one of my suits, which are now so old and threadbare I keep expecting them to split dangerously whenever I sit down on a chair. (To which the obvious response is 'Well, don't sit down on a chair, then.')

What I think we need here is a handy cut-out-and-keep-somewhere-on-your-desk-until-one-day-you-tidy-up-then-throw it-away guide to what a man of a certain age can and cannot wear. Good luck.

---

* I am reminded, not for the first time, of that most useful acronym for mad midlife cyclists: MAMIL, which stands for Middle-Aged Man in Lycra.

- Shorts: NO.
- Sandals (with socks): Absolutely not.
- T-shirt: Not outside the house, if you please.
- Short-sleeved shirts: OK if you're on holiday (especially in Hawaii) but otherwise to be avoided if you have weedy upper arms (hem hem).
- Linen shirts and trousers: YES but need ironing first.
- Jeans with jacket: OK if you don't mind looking like Jeremy Clarkson. In my neck of the woods, it's the uniform of local spivs who chat up barmaids before going home to 'the wife'.
- Fleece: Are you a sheep? Then shut up.
- Casual Wembley jumpers: As worn by TV football pundits on the morning of the FA Cup final. NO.
- Wacky Christmas jumper: Looked OK on Colin Firth in *Bridget Jones's Diary* but that doesn't mean it will look good on you. Unambiguous NO.
- Football shirt: Is your last name Maradona? It isn't? Then absolutely NO.

A few brief words about hairstyles. Baldies, who by this age are very much in the majority, have fewer options here, as you might expect. The full Lex Luthor cueball shave is fine if you have strong, even vulgar features like Telly Savalas, who became an unlikely sex symbol (to everyone but him) in the mid-1970s by shaving off all his hair and sucking lollies. I think it works less well for men with smaller, more delicate features, like Patrick Stewart, who just look like they are trying too hard. For such men, a small airstrip around the back is best left to indicate that while you have bugger-all hair now, you did once have some and you are not entirely past displaying what little you have left. Obviously combovers are never coming back into fashion, and the swirly Donald Trump method of baldness denial just makes you look silly and try-hard. If it has all gone, you are so much better off cutting it short and forgetting about it.

If you are lucky enough to still have your hair, or (like me) most of it (I'm beginning to thin, but not fast enough to start worrying about it), you have more options. Although mullets have trumped combovers and come back into fashion, the rule is simple: if you are old enough to remember them from last time, you're too old to have one. It's strictly a young person's hairstyle, for the mental distress engendered by being young today is the only real qualification. Do you see Michael Bolton or Billy Ray Cyrus growing back their mullets? Has Bono reactivated his? They have not and he has not. Do not even consider it.

Ponytails and other long hair styles are increasingly acceptable, though, partly because it sticks two fingers up to the baldies, but also because it demonstrates a certain freedom, possibly even liberation from conventional norms, and indeed Conventional Norms, who always ask for a short back and sides and would prefer that you did too. My friend Alan is now completely white but grew a rather fetching topknot that his wife simply adored. Why not? He is retired and he answers to no one, other than his wife, of course. He is no fool, and neither, obviously, is she.

16

Gammon

This is by far my favourite neologism of the past few years, better even than 'omnishambles', better even than 'pomnishambles' (what Australians say when England lose an Ashes series to them in depressingly short order). Someone noticed that most of the angriest and most vocal middle-aged men of a certain right-wing stripe had bright gammon-red faces when the steam was truly coming out of their ears, and so the word 'gammon' was coined to describe them. The age of sixty must represent some sort of peak of gammonhood, when the anger is uncontrollable but your physical strength has not yet failed you. My friend Francis took me out for lunch with a couple of gammon friends of his, both of whom moaned incessantly about anything 'woke', about left-wing cancel culture in universities, and about the way they and their kind were always silenced by the liberal elites. Speaking as a card-carrying member of the liberal elite, I couldn't have silenced them if I had hit them both round the head with a garden spade. For people who consider themselves 'silenced', they never stopped talking. They were both fervent Brexiteers

and believed that civilisation would fall if a Labour government were ever elected again. As the conversation – or rather
duologue, because neither Francis nor I could get a word in
edgeways – progressed, their faces grew redder and redder,
and one of them at least looked on the verge of a serious stroke
or maybe even keeling over with a heart attack, caused by
accumulated rage, minimal exercise over several decades and
far too many enormous lunches. This was some months ago.
I hope they're both still alive. I must ask Francis.

Gammons are everywhere, but many of them congregate
in pubs and restaurants to address other gammons in small,
but unusually noisy, groups. If they are not deaf already, they
usually become so from having right-wing drivel screamed in
their ears at top volume. I think it must be a bit like going to a
Black Sabbath gig without earplugs. No gammon ever talks at
a normal volume, because that would feel like being 'silenced'
for them. Also, not shouting would lessen the chances of your
skin going that nice pink colour, and of your heart deciding
to give up the ghost halfway through dessert. Their favourite phrases include 'I'm not a racist, but ... ', 'I'm not an
antisemite, but ... ' and 'I'm not saying Donald Trump was
right, but ... ' Everything makes them angry: women (possibly except for their 'lady wives'), blacks, Jews, foreigners
generally, the Irish, the traffic on the roads, black bus drivers
wearing sunglasses, the Labour Party, the unions, the Greens,
vegetarians, vegans, hippies, punks, mods, scooters, mods
riding scooters, Channel 4, the BBC, especially the *Today
Programme*, the *Guardian* (which they would have forcibly
closed down), students, academics, journalists, anyone who
lives in Stoke Newington, anyone who works in 'compliance'
or 'sustainability' (whatever they are), social workers, social

workers' clients, Muslims, Muslim women wearing burkas, Muslim social workers wearing burkas, Remainers (whom they call 'Remoaners'), babies, small children, big children, adolescents, gays, lesbians, trans women, trans men, trans children, drag queens, anyone who favours the pronoun 'they', actors, actresses (except for Judi Dench), actresses who call themselves 'actors', anyone who works for a charity, anyone who benefits from a charity and anyone who earns less than £50,000 a year. They glean most of their opinions from right-wing newspapers, LBC, TalkSport, other gammons and the drivers of black cabs, whom they believe to embody the Unfiltered Voice of the Working Man. ('That'll be £54.20, guv. Yes, I take cards.') Gammons have said it all before and they will say it all again, only more loudly next time. They know you are not listening, but they do not care: they will not be silenced! They do not believe in science, which they think is a con to fool the gullible. Accordingly, they do not believe in man-made climate change, not least because most of them are of an age where it will not greatly affect them. On the contrary, they think it would be rather fun if some of the world's greatest wines were grown in Kent and Sussex and the wild rugged coast of Scotland became the new Côte d'Azur. And if Australia became uninhabitable, who would care other than a few million Australians? Just as long as they didn't come over here, with their boomerangs and their hyper-aggressive sportsmen and their shrimps on the barbie. They could go to Germany. Everyone could go to Germany. Gammons hark back to an ideal British past, when Britannia ruled the waves and Germany lost the Second World War and the World Cup in quick succession. They idolise Winston Churchill and Margaret Thatcher, and admire such current figures of fun as Piers Morgan, Jeremy Clarkson and Jordan Peterson, the Canadian professor who inspired armies of weedy, fat and prematurely bald incel boys and turned himself into a scourge of the woke. The brilliant parodist Craig Brown, when writing fake diary entries for Margaret Thatcher back in the 1980s and 1990s, started and ended each of her tsunami-like rants with the phrase 'If you'd just let me finish ... ' This could be the catchphrase of many of the gammons I know.

Oddly enough, I also know one or two left-wing gammons, whose line of attack might not be the same, but whose worldview – everything is shit, except for me – is roughly equivalent.

Where does all this rage come from? I realise that modern life is incredibly annoying, and that much of the time it seems as though the whole world is trying to do you down, and while not all of it is, some of it certainly is. Banks that keep you on hold for half an hour, delivery drivers who never appear, let alone in the six-hour window you have to stay in for, and my particular bugbear, idiots who stand at pedestrian crossings and never press the button to stop the traffic, either because they haven't figured out the cause-and-effect consequence of this action, or because they know that sooner or later someone else will come and do it for them. Websites that lead you into feedback loops from which there is no escape, barbers who don't give you the haircut you want and indeed asked for, cats who wee in inappropriate places around the house, dogs that pull off your socks and lick your toes, ready meals that you cook as instructed but are still stone cold in the middle, pubs that insist on credit card payments when you only have cash ... OK, I recognise we are getting a bit niche here, but I am only trying to illustrate that wherever you turn, someone is treating you without the respect which, surely now, after all these years, you are due. When you were younger people shat all over you but somehow you put up with it, and if you didn't, those years you spent in Wormwood Scrubs will surely have persuaded you of the folly of your actions. But now you're older, fatter and uglier, you need people to do what you have told them to do and do it right now, without complaint or hesitation. If I ask for no mayonnaise on my burger, I don't actually expect no mayonnaise on my burger – I'm not that daft – but I do hope, against the odds and all experience, that there will be no mayonnaise on my burger. But seven out of ten times there is, so I send it back, whereupon the kitchen staff spit on my burger, or maybe wee on it, and it comes back with the mayonnaise crudely scraped off. I should have ordered the lasagne. I should always have ordered the lasagne.

My gammon friends have shorter fuses than they once did, and pretty much anything will set them off. As time goes on and they get into their gammony stride, they love to hate and live to rant, which actually makes them increasingly dull company. Their opinions, it is clear, have been formed and are now set in stone. They would no more change their minds than change their hairstyles, or shoes, or genitals. The few Brexiteer friends I have who have since changed their minds and now regard the whole shitshow as an unforced error of calamitous proportions, are all women. The men are as stubborn (and wrong) as you would expect. In fact these are the two qualities that all gammons, of whatever political persuasion, share. Immense stubbornness, to the point that they see their lack of doubt as a strength, when it's clear to everyone else that the inability to change your mind is a fundamental structural weakness. And, frankly, they are almost always wrong about everything. I have a gammon friend who is a climate change denier. It isn't happening because he doesn't like the idea and he doesn't want it to, because he doesn't want to change his lifestyle and because he really likes going on holiday four times a year to far-flung resorts that will be completely underwater in ten years' time. The same gammon believes that Trump was cheated in the 2020 US presidential election, because there is no way he could have lost to a wishy-washy Democrat with an obvious hair transplant. I say to him, remember the 2016 EU referendum? We Remainers lost, and all the Brexiteer gammons went about shouting 'You lost! Suck it up!' Because now the NHS would be paid £350 million more a week and we would be free to forge lavish new trade deals with Papua New Guinea and Azerbaijan. When my gammon friend starts going on about Trump, I shout 'You lost! Suck it up!' and he looks completely confused. If he wants something to be true and says it's true, then in what remains of his mind after years working in the City, it *is* true, even if it's palpable bollocks. I must ask him what he thinks of vaccinations . . .

A notch or two below the gammon state, we find simple grumpiness. My friend J complains that her husband is constantly low-level grumpy: there's nothing on the telly, ever, anywhere, the weather's shit and life has certainly lost its flavour, even though he left it on the bedpost overnight. In fact J has solved this particular conundrum in one sense, in that she has worked out that there's nothing actually wrong with her husband's life at all. He has some money, his work is interesting and he and she and their children are all fit and well. They have rebuilt their house almost from scratch and it is now a masterpiece of the interior designer's art. They go on several holidays a year, which reminds me of Paul McCartney saying that he always writes his best songs when away on holiday. 'Away on holiday from what, precisely?' is the question that instantly begs itself, but Paul is a busy man, with businesses to run, music to make, hair to dye and so forth. But J's husband hasn't anything to complain about, either: really, nothing. Not that this stops him complaining. Are we out of stamps again? These scissors are too blunt. We're about to run out of tea bags.

My own feeling is that this sort of low-level grumpiness is essentially a habit rather than anything more pathological. Familiarity, as we know, breeds contempt, but so do comfort and ease of life and the fucking scissors going blunt again. No stamps? Go to the post office and buy some. I myself grew up in a one-parent family, and my mother was always too preoccupied by my father's vengeful attempts to get us chucked out of the family home to worry about stamps, so there never were any. Nor were there paper clips, rubber bands or staples in the house, a strange result of which being that I am never without these now that I am a grown-up and know where the nearest three stationery shops are to my flat. Actually, I diligently reuse paper clips many times over, pick up the postie's discarded rubber bands from the pavement and have only bought staples once since I left my last office job in 1988 with my briefcase bulging with stolen stationery, as everyone's always is. My mother still hasn't any stamps, or greetings cards, or pens less than thirty years old, but obviously that is not my problem any more.

Grumpiness, then, is a choice, and usually a poor one. After all, where is it going to get you? Your put-upon partner isn't suddenly going to say, I've bought some new scissors, or I went to the post office today and bought three thousand first-class stamps, which should last us a while. No, she's going to seethe quietly and then, when you eventually die of your grumpiness-induced heart attack or stroke, she will (a) dance on your grave, and then (b) spend the money you leave her on marcel-waved gigolos on the French riviera. Because she will have realised that the only reason she was so grumpy all the time was that you were there too, grumbling away because someone bought the wrong breakfast cereal again. I said Ricicles, not Rice Krispies, because they are twicicle as nicicle, as any fule kno.

The genuinely disadvantaged, by contrast, do not have the room or the money to be grumpy: it's a disease of the affluent, the well-fed, the owner of the large car speeding down side roads looking for oldsters to run over. The genuinely disadvantaged are too busy trying to make ends meet, ends that will never meet however hard they try, ends that just seem to get further apart every day. You may feel underlyingly grumpy in that situation – I certainly have done when my financial situation has been parlous – but you feel the need to put on a happy face for your family and for those friends who haven't yet deserted you, tired as they are of your constant complaints about money. Grumpiness, though, seems to be an affliction of the roundly comfortable, the well-padded, the monied, the sublimely unbothered. And if you put your mind to it, it is curable.

The first solution is what people used to call a positive mental attitude. Think happy thoughts. If there's a problem, solve it yourself. Do it without complaint, and don't make the person you deal with behind the counter miserable either. Open your eyes to the beauty of the world. Hug a tree. Say a cheery 'What ho!' to every passing cat. Leave big tips in restaurants. Say thank you to everyone. Even your family members.

The second thing is therapy, which is useful in itself (for solving problems you may not know you had), but also for making you realise that most of your problems are completely trivial, now you have bought some tea bags and had the scissors sharpened.

The third is exercise. The grumpy are often the lazy and the overweight, the people who drive everywhere, even to the post office to buy stamps. Shame on you! Don't even try to deny it. Just go for a long walk, and if you end up in the pub by yourself with a book, as I often seem to, you at least have got yourself breathing and thinking and not fretting about nothing, because fresh air is not only miraculous, it's completely free, at least for the moment. (I wouldn't be at all surprised if the Conservatives have plans to privatise it, sell it to their mates, and have you paying £10 on your credit card whenever you put your shoes on.) Above all, do not run. You are too old to run, and all you will do as you jog slowly and desperately along the pavement is interest passing ambulances and terrify small children. 'Mummy, Mummy, is that old man about to die?' 'Yes, dear, and probably before he reaches the end of the road.'

The fourth is kindness. As we all know intellectually, but sometimes fail to live up to in the hurly-burly of modern life, kindness makes the world go round. Be nice to people and they will be nice to you in return. Grumpiness, by contrast, begets grumpiness, if not blunt instruments and forks in the thigh. It would be an exaggeration to say that my friend J is seriously thinking of killing her grumpy husband in cold blood, but she is beginning to wonder what actual use he is around the house, what vital function does he perform. Once the kids' school fees have been paid, I suspect he might be out on his ear.

Before then, though, she needs to say to him, Why the fuck are you so grumpy all the time? You have literally nothing to be grumpy about. Perhaps he has ended up in the grumpy place without really meaning to. Maybe under that stern and disapproving exterior lurks a heart of gold. I wouldn't put money on it, though. I suspect that a grumpy heart is like an onion: underneath the first layer of grumpiness lies a second layer of grumpiness, and so on all the way down, to a molten core of pure grumpiness. But I could be wrong. Mr J could, at heart, by an ocean of sweetness and light, and never having met him, I simply don't know. But whenever I myself feel grumpiness coming on, I now make an enormous mental effort to avert it. I ask myself, Why am I grumpy? A real reason: a tooth hurting, or an enormous cheque hasn't arrived? Or a silly, small reason: no clean underpants, or no smooth peanut butter in the cupboard? 'Eat crunchy!' is my war-cry in such circumstances, and it should be yours too.

17

News Update

My mum rang this morning and told me she has breast cancer. She had noticed some odd puckering on her left nipple, and even before she had been in for tests she knew she had it, having more medical encyclopaedias in her home than is entirely decent (have I mentioned her penchant for medical encyclopaedias?). She is ninety-one, so she is too old and fragile for surgery, and she says she is not undergoing chemotherapy as too many friends of hers have been down that route, but apparently there is a course of pills she can take. On some people the pills work very well. They don't get rid of the cancer, but they put a shield around it and stop it growing. On other people they do not work at all. I told her the Simon Gray story from the end of Chapter 1 and she laughed mirthlessly. She is actually being incredibly stoical about it all. She says she has had a good life, and things could have been so much worse. If she had got this when she was seventy-one, she would have been thoroughly pissed off. But ninety-one ... pah! She says she'd take cancer over dementia any day.

Polly and I stand in the kitchen and talk about it. If

anything, she is more upset than I am, but then I have been imagining my mother dying every day for at least ten years, and whenever I call her on the phone and she doesn't answer, it's all I can do not to ring for an ambulance. (Which wouldn't be strictly necessary if she's just gone out to buy a pint of milk.) 'Is this what life is now?' says Polly. We remember a time when the phone would ring and you would think, Goody, the phone's ringing, I do hope it's someone interesting. As opposed to now, when you think, what new disaster has befallen one of my loved ones? So I said yes, this is what life is now. People are going to fall ill and many of them will die.

My mum says she has outlived all her old friends and a lot of her family. Cousins from the next generation down are beginning to croak. She isn't afraid of death, she says: the man with the scythe has been trailing around behind her for a while now, especially when she visits Selfridges, where he is known to hang around the perfume section. And if she dies now, or rather, quite soon, she won't have to worry about becoming immobile and being unable to go up or down stairs, which, as she lives on the first floor, has been a concern for some time now. She won't have to worry about being put in a care home, which she would hate. It means that, to an extent, she will go out of the world on her terms. Ill, hospice, morphine, death. I think she'd still prefer a massive heart attack on her 107th birthday, as obviously would I, for her and for me, but this is probably the next best thing.

What will happen to her tiny and astoundingly ill-tempered dog, Penelope? As it happens, Penelope just celebrated her twelfth birthday, probably by licking someone's toes, so she is coming to the end as well, and my mother says she has seen a dog holding a scythe following them round Regent's Park. I am not a fan of dogs on the whole, and Penelope's shortness of temper, tendency to bark whenever my mother is not applying her full attention to her and breath so poisonous it can melt plastic are not strong recommendations for future owners. I would favour the pillow-over-the-face method myself, but I imagine a more gentle means of exit will be found.

I ask my mum whether she would not prefer the pillow-over-the-face method for herself. She laughs, even more mirthlessly than before.

As it happens, yesterday afternoon Polly went for a routine mammogram in a tent in Morrisons car park in Borehamwood. She has cancelled this twice before because she was afraid of what the result would be, despite no lumps in her breasts or obvious problems with them. She says the worst thing that could happen is that about a week afterwards she will get a phone call on her mobile from 'Unknown Caller', which will turn out to be a doctor telling her that there's an anomaly in the mammogram and she needs to have a biopsy. 'And then I'll be on cancer highway,' she says, as though it's already happened. I tell her the chances of her and my mother having breast cancer at exactly the same moment are vanishingly small, but she rejects all probability and common sense and is fully expecting to die, maybe as soon as next week.

Meanwhile, I go out for lunch with my friend Bethen, who has been spending a lot of time by the side of her father, who is dying of pancreatic cancer at home in the Midlands. She saw him in May, thought, There's something not quite right about you, he was diagnosed in June and now, in November, he is at most days away from death. He was a big, burly bloke when I met him, big-faced with loads of charm and a twinkle in his eye. Now, apparently, he is skin and bone. Last week he could get out of bed to go to the loo. This week, no. The pain has become intolerable, so he is now tripping on morphine, and has become convinced that there's a tiny man living on the ceiling, hiding in the corner of the room. While we're eating, Bethen's stepmother calls her to say that he is now unequivocally on the way out, and she needs to go up as soon as possible. But Bethen can't face it or him or the rest of the extended step-family, so we drink all afternoon, and well into the evening. She will go up tomorrow, she says, already contemplating the giant hangover that will be accompanying her.

My mother rings up again. She has been to the hospital to discuss the options. Surgery and chemotherapy are definitely out, although radiotherapy is still a possibility. If the pills work she might have five more years. As she said, 'I don't know that I've got five more years anyway, so I'm pretty happy with that.'

I had lunch with Bethen on Tuesday. On Friday her father died. She was with him at the end.

My old friend Judy (we went out with each other for nine months in 1979: yes, that old) contacts me to tell me that her beloved husband Adrian died of cancer on Monday. Another one! I hadn't even known he was ill! He was at most two or three years older than me, and such a nice and gentle man.

No news on the mammogram yet – and no news is almost certainly good news – but Polly had a piercing pain down her right side over the weekend and went to have a blood test to see if there was something nasty lurking in there. The blood test showed nothing out of the ordinary, and her urgent face-to-face follow-up appointment with her GP was downgraded to not-so-urgent. We breathe again, even if several people we know do not.

18

Stuff

What do you want for Christmas? It's 24 December, I have wrapped all the presents I am giving and am faintly apprehensive about what I myself shall receive tomorrow. Because these days, when asked what I want, I can never think of anything. 'Wine,' I usually say, or 'chocolate', or 'a decent jigsaw'. Books I have more than enough of, especially now that I have started re-reading books I first read thirty or forty years ago. Clothes I don't really need, although I could probably do with a new pair of shoes, as one of my two operative pairs has a hole in the side that can't be repaired. I have one really good coat and one acceptable one, I have two suits (one dark, for funerals and winter, the other light, for posh parties and summer), I have three dressing gowns (one for winter, one for summer, one intermediate) and I have five scarves, two bought by me, three given as Christmas presents by people who gave me gloves the previous year (even though I never wear gloves and they always go straight to the charity shop). We have enough vases, more than enough mugs (which for some reason never break), not quite enough wine glasses (which break all the time), enough saucepans and the right number of small jugs (three) that sit on the kitchen windowsill looking pretty but performing no practical role whatsoever. We have enough knives and forks, more spoons that anyone could feasibly use and several corkscrews. We don't have enough pairs of scissors, it's true, and we must address this at some point. But everywhere in this smallish flat there is stuff. My stuff, Polly's stuff, the children's stuff, family stuff. We are drowning in stuff, and every bag of stuff we take to the charity shop or the dump makes not the slightest bit of difference. Like many writers I have a pile of old newspapers sitting in the corner, which provide the reading matter in the loo and then finally disappear to be recycled or to protect the brutal shards of yet another broken wine glass in the rubbish. Do I actually need these newspapers? No. Do I ever look at them, other than to do all the puzzles I never got round to doing while half-watching *Pointless* on BBC iPlayer? No. (Mine is an incredibly exciting life.)

There's the cat's cardboard box on the floor, because every cat in the world would rather sit in a ratty old cardboard box than anywhere else, and there's the cat's other cardboard box next to it, because he likes a bit of variety. There's the piano, now rarely played, and never tuned. There are pictures on the wall, and curtains at the window and a crappy old sofa we got for free on Freecycle, and an armchair and my grandmother's oak dining table, and five chairs around it, only two of which can be sat on by people weighing more than six stone. And books, books, books everywhere: books I loved, books I didn't much care for but haven't quite got round to getting rid of, reference books I have only opened twice, books by friends I can't get rid of, books given to me (and inscribed) by friends, some of whom have since died, books I might read again, and others I shall never read again, under any circumstances.

And we wouldn't even consider ourselves hoarders. I'm not one of those sad men wearing fingerless gloves who have hoarded so many newspapers and magazines they have to climb over sheaves of them to get to the loo in the morning, an effort so enormous sometimes they don't quite make it in time ...

When my grandmother died, nearly thirty years ago, my mother had to go through all her possessions, throw some in the bin, sell what could be sold and take the rest to the charity shop. Amongst her belongings was what amounted to a large cardboard box of toby jugs, which were all utterly repulsive and, it transpired, completely worthless. The charity shops refused to take them. 'No resale value,' they explained. Similarly, my old friend Chris, when he was clearing out his parents' house, found two complete sets of *Encyclopaedia Britannica*, one from the 1960s, one more recent. Resale value: nil. Both toby jugs and encyclopaedias eventually went into landfill, although some enterprising soul could probably have lagged a loft or two with the latter. My nearest charity shop told me last week that they would no longer take CDs. 'No one wants them any more,' they explained. 'Vinyl we've got room for,' they added, but I had to let them down gently, as I had just flogged a huge pile of terrible old records to the second-hand vinyl shop that has opened up next to Sainsbury's. Vinyl has value again whereas compact discs do not: many of my friends who hauled their own record collections to charity shops fifteen or twenty years ago are wishing they had just put them in the loft, as I did, though in my case it was through indolence and inertia rather than ingenious foresight.

We all have too many things, and although I don't go as far as Marie Kondo, who is clearly deranged, there must be good sense in getting rid of what we no longer want or need. I have probably written my last cricket book – I have now done five, which I think is enough – and I realised that more than forty years of *Wisden Cricketers' Almanack* were taking up space that could easily be filled by other books. I remain quite proud of the collection but it's like the newspapers: do I ever look at them? Do I love them still as I once did? The answer to both questions is no, so out they must go. I have tried giving them to cricket-crazed friends of mine, who it turns out have either got rid of their own collections or have every edition since 1910 lining the walls of their garage. I thought I could sell them on eBay, and I might still do so, but they are all but worthless, even my oldest editions, from 1977 and 1979. I shall keep the nine or ten editions to which I contributed pieces, but the rest have outlived their usefulness.

Have you seen my desk recently? Neither have I, because it's covered with shit. Old newspapers I haven't yet done the puzzles in, books I never finished reading, old quizzes, piles and piles and piles of filing I must get round to doing some-day. Somewhere under there is a pair of scissors I lost six months ago. (I hope.)

Old pieces of paper, written or printed on on one side, are reused as 'rough' paper. Vast piles of dead ink cartridges sit on the shelf because I know they can be recycled but I'm not entirely sure how. One day I shall find out, and then they will be gone too, put in one of the many used jiffy bags I am also trying to recycle, and failing, because jiffy bags definitely reproduce. They feed on all the used bubble wrap I also put down the side of my desk. There should be enough bubble wrap down there to safely pack a cathedral for first-class post, but it has all vanished, and when I need some I will certainly have to go and buy it. Jiffy bags, I suspect, are the apex predators in the stationery jungle. Maybe it was they who ate the scissors I lost six months ago.

If we ever go anywhere outside London we have to unload from the boot of the car all the old clothes and no-longer-functional electric equipment Polly was planning to take to the dump. When we come back we have to put it all back in again. There's one old pair of boots I swear has been there for YEARS. (Unless they have been reproducing too. I suspect they have dined on the plastic bag full of dead batteries that has been hiding in there under the ancient road map of France since 2016.)

And yet we all still go shopping to buy more stuff. Actually, I don't much any more, although I'll shop for food and drink and books, the essentials. I'll buy presents for people, and cards to send out whenever I remember (which isn't often), and stamps to quell the stamp-shaped childhood trauma referred to previously, and toothbrushes (because I am, for some reason, the person who buys the family toothbrushes), but very little else, because shopping is both unspeakably horrible and a waste of life (and money). In 2011 Renata Salecl, a Slovenian philosopher and theorist, published a book called *The Tyranny of Choice*. She believes that choice 'brings a sense of overwhelming responsibility into play, and this is bound up with a fear of failure, a feeling of guilt and an anxiety that regret will follow if we make the wrong choice'. This is how most shopping feels to me. Barry Schwartz is a psychologist and social theory professor, who gave a TED Talk in 2005 in which he explained that 'an explosion of choice' has led affluent Western societies towards 'paralysis rather than liberation'. He talked about his local store stocking 175 types of salad dressing, and about the time he went to buy a new pair of jeans and was paralysed by all the different styles and fits. With so many choices to be made in everyday life, Schwartz argued that humans increasingly find it difficult to choose at all, and when they do, they are rarely satisfied with their decision. They're haunted by the lingering thought of other options they could have chosen. His talk has been viewed sixteen million times.

Polly has recently spent entire days trying to shop online for a lampshade, finally finding one that she liked enough to buy, and then establishing that it was out of stock. 'Wait a little,' I said. 'It'll come back into stock sooner or later and then you pounce.' A week later it did come back into stock. If I order it now, reasoned Polly, I'll get it on Thursday, but I want it now. There was a shop, actual bricks and mortar, selling these things about four miles away, so she got into her car and drove there, only to find that they didn't have any of the particular one she liked. By the time she had driven back and looked online again, the lampshade was out of stock again.

Ten years ago, I wrote about the joy of recycling, which has brightened the lives of many a middle-aged man of thrifty habit. Empty wine bottles, certain robust plastics, newspapers, old bits of aluminium foil: they all go into the great green plastic bag which goes outside our flat on a Tuesday morning, which is then collected by the cheery operatives of the private company now hired by our borough to collect all our waste, who then chuck it in the back of the rubbish lorry and secretly bury it in landfill when no one is looking, with all the dead mobile phones and cat poo, and the millions of old cabbages thrown out by Sainsbury's every day. Or maybe they export it to impoverished countries where it is burnt for fuel. I don't know and I don't care. My responsibility ends with the placing of these items in the great green plastic bag, and while I'd like to think that they are all recycled for the great good of humankind, I'm not so naive to think that they actually are, or that there's anything I can do about it if they aren't. I have come to think of recycling as a great middle-class fantasy, which makes us feel nice and valued and useful while not letting us be any of these things. In that sense recycling has become a metaphor for life itself. We all want to be better than we are and here's one way we can actually appear to be, while not actually being at all, at almost no effort. I'm all for no effort, even if the end result is that you achieve nothing.

So the charity shop runs continue. 'Anything for the charity shop?' I bawl upstairs, and my daughter comes down with a few books she doesn't need or want and a few items of clothing she borrowed from friends and can't be arsed to return. My son grunts non-committally and goes back to sleep, and Polly points to a pile of books that are mine and that she doesn't want around the house any more. No, they're sacrosanct, I explain, with the patience of a saint. I might pop a few of hers in the bag when she's not looking, and in return she will find my plastic bag full of old leads (all superseded by more current leads) and put it in the boot of the car to be taken, one day, to the dump. It's a war of attrition and there are no winners, other than the jiffy bags still reproducing noisily down the side of my desk.

19

Pottering

My friend Terence has been pottering, unashamedly, since we were both at university, more than forty years ago. He can potter for Britain. I asked him to define the term. He looked thoughtful for a moment and then said, 'Action without notable achievement.' I said, would you count emptying the bins or taking the rubbish out as pottering? Or paying some bill online? Of course, he said. Well, in my book, I said, I count all of those as considerable achievement. Have you ever wondered whether you should get out more? said Terence.

Pottering at twenty, though, has a different texture from pottering at sixty. At twenty it's a lifestyle choice. You may still be living at home, and constantly having parents telling you to clean your room, which you only do to your own, very specific (not very hygienic) requirements. Or if you are sharing a flat, it is probably a pit of the utmost degradation, never cleaned, with dirty plates and mugs everywhere, something more from one of the outer circles of Dante's Hell than from recognisable normal life. My brother has spoken to me of his gradual transformation from, at heart, one of the Young Ones to a clean-and-tidy freak of terrifying proportions, someone who regularly hoovers behind furniture that in other houses (mine, for example) may not have been moved for years, if not decades. Here is a man who always cleans the bath out, not just when guests are coming over, and who always unloads the dishwasher before reading the paper. But this isn't pottering. This is the manic activity of a diseased mind (sorry, bro).

Pottering at twenty means doing things that probably don't need to be done at all. Moving books from one shelf to another, or moving plants from one table to another. Pottering at sixty, though, is the very stuff of life. It's going to make a cup of tea (or coffee) at exactly the same time every day. It's doing the Killer Sudoko puzzle on the back page of the *Guardian*, and when you finally complete it you feel as elated as if you had run 10k. It's making the bed, ironing a shirt, filing some paperwork (although I think the last only counts if it has lain in your filing tray, untouched and unconsidered, for several months). It's pottering if you have a bath or shower not because you strictly need one (because you had one last night or this morning) but just because you feel like one. Pottering is if you go out to buy some milk but return with a family pack of Minstrels as well, almost by mistake. (These are mistakes I seem to make frequently.) Making a snack for yourself is pottering, whereas making a snack for someone else is either love or drudgery (or both). Golf and bridge are pottering given structure; competitive pottering, if you prefer. Gardening is pottering al fresco: either you're taking out weeds (plants you don't want) or installing plants you do want, but in the long run, unless you're Monty Don, all gardening is essentially pointless, as you are always fighting a losing battle against an irresistible force, the glorious, random fecundity of Mother Nature. Reading a book in a chair is an outlying region of pottering, but only if you go to sleep and start snoring like a beached whale. In fact, at sixty, almost all activity is pottering, as long as it doesn't achieve much. I'd say going for a run amounts to pottering, but only if you shamble along the road like an old wreck, and not if you have decent running shoes and actually lift your feet off the pavement. Driving is only pottering if you don't have anywhere to go, or if you are taking things to the dump, especially if you turn up at the dump and realise you have left them at home by mistake.

Collecting dead batteries for recycling is classic pottering, especially if you have no idea how or where to recycle them. Buying things online isn't pottering, but forgetting you have done so and then being surprised when they turn up a few days later is. Going shopping to a real bricks-and-mortar shop isn't pottering either, unless you go straight to the café and buy tea and cake. Going for a walk is pottering, unless you are one of those maniacs who needs to walk at full speed around a park to show everyone how fit and dedicated you are. (File that one under mental illness, too, I'm afraid.) Wandering up to your local bookshop on a sunny afternoon, as I plan to do after lunch today, is Premier League pottering, whether you buy a book or not (but if you do buy one, you probably have to go to a coffee shop afterwards to look at it and sniff the virgin pages and stroke the spine lovingly, as I do). Going to any off-licence is definite pottering, albeit pottering with a purpose, which is a bit like pottering with a porpoise but altogether drier, usually. Writing this chapter is very nearly pottering, as my mind is jumping from subject to subject as though someone has plugged it into the mains. I blame this on the three cups of tea I have just drunk, at the same time of day that I always drink three cups.

Reading this chapter, though, is definite pottering, because you could probably do almost anything else at all and achieve more. The essence of pottering is that whatever you are doing doesn't truly need to be done, or at least not right now. So paying a bill on deadline (or after, when you start to incur charges) is just pure stress, whereas paying it way in advance is pure pottering, whether or not you have the funds in the bank with which to pay it. My friend Terence, referred to earlier, has married a woman who seems to like pottering nearly as much as he does. She is constantly adjusting her bookshelves, or redecorating the spare room when it doesn't really need redecorating. They are very happy indeed.

20

News Update II

Polly's mammogram was completely clear. But now she has a brutal pain down her left-hand side, ending with an even more brutal pain in her bowel. 'Is it bowel cancer?' she asks me. 'No,' I say.

My old friend Bill* keeled over with a massive stroke not so long ago. 'Are you in pain?' asked his sister, who found him laid out on the sitting room floor. 'No,' said Bill. The ambulance arrived within twenty minutes, and she wasn't allowed to go with him, for Covid-related reasons, so that was the last she saw of him. They operated, but the two blood clots on his brain were inaccessible, and he didn't wake up from the operation. A day or two later he was declared brain-dead, and soon after they switched off the machines keeping him 'alive'. Another sister and his best friend of fifty years were there when he died. He was eighteen months older than me.

---

* Not the same Bill who supplied those superb pop quizzes for my book *Berkmann's Pop Miscellany*, but another Bill, who for simplicity and convenience, was known as William in that book. But he was always, and very definitely, a Bill.

We were in the same form at school: he was the oldest boy, I was the youngest. So I had known him since 1972, but we were never that close. My best friends in that family were two of his (four) younger sisters. But Bill was a lovely, gentle, absurdly stubborn man, who, having started as a doctrinaire Marxist, moved towards anarchism in his early twenties and thereafter fetched up as a dedicated Christian, working regularly at a homeless shelter and becoming a stalwart of his church's community. His sister Kate said that every church needs a Bill: 'a practical man who can actually do things'. As his best friend, Richard, said at his funeral, 'he had intellect, wisdom and knowledge. It's rare to find all three in the same person.' The funeral, by the way, was glorious.

I didn't stay long at the wake, because I was wearing a ridiculous black beanie hat, to conceal my injuries from an accident a couple of days before. Having had a few at lunchtime, I tripped on the stairs and fell straight into some glass-fronted photographs that were waiting to be hung up on the wall. My face wasn't so bad but the front of my scalp looked like the Battle of the Somme. Was the accident caused by the drink (probably), or was it something to do with the way my clumsiness has increased and my sense of balance has declined? I read in *Saga Magazine* that at the age of forty, most of us can balance on one leg for forty or fifty seconds, easily, whereas at the age of sixty this is reduced to ten seconds. All I know is that it takes me rather longer than it did to put on a pair of pants in the morning, and I now have to lean against something, normally a wall, to make it less effortful. Is this general age-related decline or is it a warning of something more serious: Parkinson's maybe, or (sweating while typing this) motor neurone disease? Right now, I don't want to find out. As my daughter put it when I told her about the age-related decline in balance detailed above, 'Well, don't stand on one leg then.'

Polly's stomach pains have eased, at last, after twelve days. My mum looked it up in her medical encyclopaedia, and diagnosed stress-related gastritis, possibly brought on by hearing me fall down the stairs, crash into some glass and bleed profusely all over the carpet. Makes sense to me.

I have cut down on my drinking since the accident. I have drunk too much for more years than I care to remember, but this has recently tipped over into drinking far too much, so I have decided to reduce the amount consumed from an average of a bottle of wine an evening to two-thirds of a bottle – four glasses rather than six – and also an entirely drink-free evening at least once a week. Already I am sleeping better and snoring less, especially after the drink-free evenings, which means fewer jabs in the ribs from my put-upon partner and not quite so many otherwise unexplainable bruises all over my body. (And after a drink-free evening, you look forward so much to the wine you're going to drink the next evening it's almost slightly pathetic.)

As for my worries about Parkinson's, my friend Paul was diagnosed with it at the age of forty-nine, which certainly qualifies as 'early-onset' (a more normal age to contract the bugger would be ... sixty). Three years on, he certainly has the 'Parkinson's gait', which is leaning forward as though carrying a rucksack full of boulders, and shuffling along in small steps rather than walking along with large, comfortable strides. Billy Connolly was in a Hollywood supermarket when a passing doctor noticed that he was moving in this way, and went up to him and said, have you seen a doctor about that? Connolly hadn't, and when he did he was diagnosed too.

Even though there's no evidence that I myself have Parkinson's, I read up about it obsessively. My mother even reads up about it in her giant medical encyclopaedia. She is feeling guilty about the six bottles of red wine she gave me for Christmas, and that she is solely responsible for turning me into the sort of desperate alcoholic who falls down stairs and crashes into glass. 'Cheers!' say I, ironically.

21

Memories

We think we remember everything, but we do not. A while ago my old friend Hilary (who was my girlfriend when we were in our teens) unearthed a fragment of diary she had written in 1978, when she was sixteen going on seventeen and I was just over a year older. After she had edited and shaped it for public consumption, she sent it round to a select few of us who might still be interested, and I read it with fascination. I can safely say that I remember nothing of what was detailed in this diary, nothing at all. It was immensely revealing, both about me and about Hilary and about some of our friends, and one has to say, some of our 'friends' (who may not have had our best interests at heart), but the actual incidents recorded I had no memory of, and the diary didn't even provoke my memory into recalling them. No, they had gone, as though they had never happened. An entire year of my life. It was both galling and fascinating to discover this.

Everybody's memory is different, but I would say that all of them, bar those of weird people who weirdly remember EVERYTHING, have some pretty big holes in them. I have one friend who remembers precisely what she was wearing on every social occasion of the past forty years, and I have another who remembers exactly what she ate at every dinner party she has been to in the same period. But does the first one remember what she ate and the second one remember what she wore? I don't imagine so. I remember that a pint of Skol in my college beer cellar in 1979 cost 65p, which was cheap even then (I think it was about £1.20 or £1.30 in a proper pub). But I don't have any recollection of any of the thousands of table football games I played there, or any of the hundreds of games of three-card brag I played there, other than to name the two people we all suspected of cheating (never proved, I'm sad to say). I can remember the college dining hall, but not why I never once went to lunch there. I can remember my rooms in college, I remember the worn stone steps outside the dining hall, I remember the purser's fat face and dodgy hairstyle, but not his name (Paul? Dave? Theosophat?). I can remember the endless feelings of discomfort and embarrassment I had when I was there, of not quite fitting in, of feeling apart from everyone else in my college and from the whole experience, except once or twice when I was probably drunk enough not to care. But why did I feel like that? Now I'm not really sure. Whenever I go back to my college for reunions I feel extremely comfortable, almost too comfortable, and absurdly happy to see everyone, the friends I made when I was there and the many others I made subsequently. Why was it so uncomfortable at the time? And why did I walk around the streets of the city with nowhere to go, hoping desperately to bump into someone I knew and almost never doing so? My need for other people must have been so much greater than my ability to make connections with them. But that's deduced from what I know now rather than what I understood then. To a great extent my past selves have become a mystery to me.

Earlier on in this book, I discussed the impossibility of going back to previous books you wrote and updating them, because each book reflected who you were at the time you wrote it and you are that person no longer. That particularly applies to people like me who write, for want of a better term, largely autobiographical non-fiction. But if you write novels, I'm sure it also applies. You can read an old novel of yours, marvel at its callowness, but also be impressed by its youthful energy and sheer drive, qualities that may since have departed. In his old age the Irish writer John McGahern went back and rewrote his old short stories, and in the process made them even more bleak and depressing than they had been originally. I quite liked the first drafts, as we must now think of them. The rewritten versions were drained of all hope, and I found them pretty much unreadable. It's possible also that in the intervening years my own tastes had changed, and that I now found his tales of rural Ireland, impoverished farmers and desolate kiddy-fiddling priests less enriching than I had before. But I still think it was wasted effort on his part. Write something new! Don't revisit the past!

My mother's conversation is interspersed with memories, like raisins in a teacake. She will say, do you remember going on holiday to Crete when you were young? I say, no, I was one and a half, and I have told you that I don't remember that holiday maybe fifty times before. Or do you remember our friends Teddy and Peggy down at Sarre Court? I say no, I was three when we visited them, I have no memory of them or their home, although I remember their names because you have mentioned them so often since. My mum remembers all these things, of course, but she never remembers that I don't remember them, and (even more annoying, this) she never remembers that I don't like Christmas pudding and that I never eat it. Do you want some? she asks every Christmas and offers me a choice of cream or custard. No, I explain with agonising patience, I don't like Christmas pudding and I never have done. Funny, that, she says, because I love it. I know you do, I reply, and you should know that I don't, because we have had exactly the same conversation every Christmas for nigh on sixty years.

Memories are fragile, and growing ever more fragile, which is probably why we end up telling the same stories again and again. My mother rang yesterday to say she had woken that morning with a completely new memory in her mind: something that had definitely happened to her but which, up till now, she had completely forgotten about. Are you sure it happened, I asked, or are you just remembering your dream? She was sure it had happened, she said, and she told me the story, which was so boring it couldn't possibly have been a dream. I said, you can probably forget that one, it's so boring, which would reduce the risk of it turning up again in normal conversation as part of her vast library of anecdotes, a risk I don't personally wish to take. She laughed and threatened to tell me the story again if I didn't shut up. You will, I said, you will.

We understand the fragility of memory ever more viscerally as we get older, as people we know start falling prey to Alzheimer's and other forms of dementia. A friend of ours, a former cricketer with my team, was diagnosed with early-onset Alzheimer's at the age of fifty-seven. A year or two later a group of us went out to lunch with him, to a Thai restaurant in Chelsea. Andy was very tanned, as bald as an egg and had an unusually unlined face, at least compared with the shambling physical wrecks surrounding him. But in the intervening time he had become a fully paid-up conspiracy theorist who saw invisible patterns in everything and underhand business everywhere. I have often thought that a fondness for conspiracy theories was evidence of dodgy mental health, and here it seemed was proof. But given his firm grasp of non-existent conspiracies in British public life, his attention was otherwise apt to wander. When my old friend Cliff said he was now working part-time for a mental health charity in Hastings, where he now lived, Andy diligently wrote notes on his paper napkin, to help him remember later. Someone happened to read the notes. 'Cliff lives in a mental asylum,' Andy had written. It was incredibly upsetting to see this lovely man, whom we had all known for the best part of thirty years, falling apart before our eyes. Worse for his family, though, and even worse for him. This is the future for some of us, we realised, as we looked round the table wondering who would be next.

What one person remembers, another person might remember very differently. I had a rather bleak illustration of this when *Zimmer Men* came out in 2005. *Rain Men* had described the internecine strife of the cricket team I was then playing for and helping to run, and *Zimmer Men* took the story on, as the team split in two and I took my half on into the great cricketing unknown. We're still playing nearly twenty years later, so we obviously did something right.

Anyway, in *Zimmer Men* I told a story, of something that had happened many years before, in a game against a team called Charlton-on-Otmoor in darkest Oxfordshire. Harry, the cricket tragic with whom I ran the original team, was fielding on the boundary at long off and took a high catch right on the boundary. Members of the opposition, sitting outside the nearby pavilion, swore that his foot had gone over the boundary line when he took the catch, which meant that it wasn't out and that the batsman had in fact scored a six. My friend Neal, fielding not far away at long on, agreed. I was fielding at mid-wicket so I couldn't see what had happened, but Harry swore blind that his foot had not crossed the boundary and that he had taken a clean catch. He was so convincing that the umpire took his word for it and gave the batsman out once again. In the book I said that what was fascinating about this was not whether or not Harry had been telling the truth – indeed, I made no judgement as to the veracity of his claim – but that years later no one remembered when this game had happened, and certainly no one could remember the result of the match, but everyone still remembered the incident and every year when we went back there to play we would all talk about it as though it had happened the previous day. Cricket, I said, is all about stories, even little ones like this, which trumps the bigger story, such as who actually won.

At around the time the book came out, Harry was diagnosed with lung cancer, even though he had never smoked. To amuse him I sent a hardback of the new book to him in hospital. He read the chapter and took it completely the wrong way. He thought I was accusing him of having cheated, which I wasn't, although I wouldn't have put it past him. (He often had a purely tangential relationship with the truth.) He wrote me a letter of such rage, enmity and viciousness that I immediately tore it up and binned it, something I have regretted ever since (especially now that I am telling this story). I remember only one line, which was something to the effect that 'you and your friends are laughing at my cancer', which couldn't have been further from the truth. Harry never spoke to me again, died in November that year (aged forty-five) and banned me from his funeral. Before he died, he wrote a book about his own cricket team's world tour the previous winter, which mentioned me and several mutual friends, not altogether kindly. I haven't read it all the way through, but I was once loitering in WHSmith in Paddington station when I saw a copy. I opened it at random and read a story about me which was completely made up and made me look weak and foolish. I put the book back on the shelf and went and caught my train.

Harry's book outsold mine by about ten to one, helped to bestsellerdom by his ridiculously premature death and by his status as the first producer of *Have I Got News for You*, among other shows. Had he not fallen ill we would have resolved the argument sooner or later, I am sure, but as things stand there are friends of his who remember me as a complete bastard and friends of mine (especially those ripped to shreds in his horrible book) who remember him the same way. All over a catch claimed in an otherwise completely forgotten cricket match. We don't even play Charlton any more: they disbanded more than a decade ago.

22

Dating

This is a big one, and there are good reasons for leaving it until the end of the book, in that it's almost certainly something you don't want to think about ever again. Remember being 'out there', and how awful it was? How lonely and dispiriting and how completely pointless, most of the time. It's at least a quarter of a century since I was 'out there' (which sounds like being in a desert without any water or even a hat), but it seems that things may have changed a touch in the intervening years. You now sell yourself on the internet as though you were a slab of meat, or someone looking for a job in marketing. People like the look of you or they don't. That is to say, they like the look of you in 2005, face retouched and wrinkles electronically removed, or they don't. They don't believe that photo of you and, frankly, neither do I. How disappointed will they be when this tiny wizened old man shuffles into the restaurant rather than the tall, broad-shouldered Adonis they quite fancied online. I'm already disappointed on their behalf, and I won't even be there. And if I am there you will really be in trouble, because I'll be sitting in your seat and you'll have no choice but to turn round and go home, back to your Pot Noodles and that episode of *Miss Marple* you have been saving for a rainy day. For there will be none rainier that this, you can be assured of that.

So although I haven't been out dating myself, I know a few people who have suffered this torment. One of the pubs near me is well known as a dating pub, and the daters always sit at the same table next to the piano. They talk to each other in that wild-eyed, slightly brittle manner that tells you they will remember absolutely nothing of what they have said, or are being told, at any point in the future. This is bad news if they actually forge some sort of relationship – we've all had those 'But I told you I was an only child' conversations. In one case she had told me that she was a non-identical twin, a fact I consumed and instantly forgot, as though I had been brainwashed by her sheer fanciability. That's my excuse, anyway. Maybe I was just too nervous or self-conscious: I was twenty-eight, for god's sake, and that's not much of an age for anything, especially listening and absorbing significant personal information.

Back to the dating pub, where the couples, or non-couples as I prefer to think of them, look at their phones nervously and wonder what drinks to order. A pint of cider? Too studenty. Most expensive bottle on the wine list? A bit flash. Ginger beer? You're either teetotal or a rampaging alcoholic who doesn't want to look like one. Funnily enough the same table next to the piano has another name: the break-up table. I have seen at least three couples have their last ever argument while sitting at this table, before one of them storms off in a huff, never to be seen again. I mentioned this to one of the bar staff, who said how funny this was as she and her boyfriend had had the most godawful row while sitting at that table, one of their worst ever. 'Don't ever sit there again,' I warned her, with the wisdom of great age. She hasn't, and when she cleans the table after people have left it's with real concentration, as though it's dirty beyond the efficacy of all cleaning fluids. Whether it is or not, it's definitely cursed, and the ghosts of all the relationships that broke down there and all the babies that were never subsequently born float around it almost visibly. Unless that's a cloud of cleaning fluid ...*

Daters are always obvious, because it's clear that they don't know each other at all, and probably never will, so much is he drinking and so much is she looking at her phone. Is she looking at his details on the dating site they both used, staring at the photo he has used of the young Brad Pitt once again, or is she checking out other blokes on there for later? Or is she texting her friend, 'I'm next to a right one here. Talks only about his car/computer/mother ... '

Another pub I go to has a reputation as an affair pub, mainly because it's out of the way but also because all the staff have told me it is. There's one couple who have been going there for so long that everyone now assumes they are married to each other, which they may well be, although obviously no one likes to ask. But apparently they are still very affectionate, which suggests that they remain married

---

* My friend Suzana, who also works at this pub, doesn't believe that couples split up at the break-up table. She thinks they just go home and have 'angry, bitter sex'. But she doesn't believe that any young people split up any more. 'Relationships just decline into situationships.' She thinks that the price of property, and come to think of it, everything else, militates against people breaking up. 'Better the devil you know,' she says, 'even if it turns out you don't really know them at all.' I find this notion unimaginably depressing.

to other people and are each other's bit on the side. We all wonder, and speculate endlessly.*

There's nothing like the icy politeness of a date that has come to an end without there being the slightest bit of 'chemistry', although that's better than when one fancies the other but the other isn't interested. I've seen and heard several conversations along the lines of 'Well, can I see you again?' 'I don't think so' although only one that went 'Well, can I see you again?' 'You've got to be fucking joking', which at least was entertaining for anyone within earshot, which was obviously everyone in the building.

The problem of the photo of Brad Pitt aged twenty-six that has somehow found itself supplanting the real-life photo of you on your profile page is one that several of my female friends have encountered more than once. Another irritant is all the usual lies about height – if you're weedy and five foot five inches in your stockinged feet, then saying you're six foot and have a chest like Dwayne 'The Rock' Johnson is to put yourself at physical risk from the righteous rage of womanhood. No jury would convict, and it's possible that other women in the pub or restaurant may join in on your savage beating. If you're ugly, and let's face it, by this age you probably are, far better to admit it than to pretend otherwise. But time and again in the dating pub, the woman (who is often there first, drinking a white wine spritzer and checking her phone) sees the special effect approaching her,

---

* Since my daughter started working at the pub up the road, I have discovered that there's no one worse than bar staff for endless speculation about the private lives of their customers. One woman, whose name is Helen, is known as 'Happy, Happy Helen' because she's always so incredibly happy, in a way they obviously find slightly offensive.

possibly holding petrol station flowers, and pulls a face that alternates between physical disgust and uncontrollable rage, a combination that suggests that this date might not be the untrammelled success she was hoping for.*

Please turn up on time. This means at least three minutes early, not rolling up half an hour late smelling of beer.

Please do not say 'I'm not like other guys'. As dating expert Justin Myers pointed out in the *Guardian*, saying this actually proves that you are like other guys, because all guys say this.

Do not talk constantly about yourself, or even worse, when she says something, instantly bring the conversation back to something you were saying earlier about yourself. Ask questions. Answer questions. One man a woman friend of mine met asked lots of questions (good) but never answered any. She eventually decided that his air of mystique was actually a feeble attempt to conceal the lack of a functional personality, or possibly a criminal record (such as the third Oasis album). Myers thinks never asking questions means he's 'hiding a grim opinion that would send you running for the hills'. Maybe he's a climate change denier or a fan of Boris Johnson or wears a Queen's Park Rangers replica kit during sex. Maybe, like the former long-term boyfriend of an old friend of mine, he's a secret cross-dresser. Everyone has secrets, but if someone knows nothing about you other than

---

* My mum has a friend who, she says, has been on literally hundreds of internet dates. She even put herself on a website for millionaires, hoping to find a rich, handsome man who could keep her in the style to which she looked forward to becoming accustomed. But all the men were fat, most were bald and many had appallingly bad breath. If you're a millionaire, fat and bald, you probably don't have valued confidants who will tell you, before you go out on a date, 'You've got breath like a donkey's arse.' More's the pity, hee hee hee.

the fact that you have secrets, you're never going to get very far with them.

Apparently, according to body-language experts, people who look up and to the right a lot might be lying. Or are the body-language experts lying? Should we look down and to the left, at the waiter's shoes, to show our palpable sincerity?

Myers says, above all, don't wear odd socks: it is a dullard's idea of a personality quirk, in the absence of any others. 'See also: cravats; unwashed hair; "I can't function without my morning espresso"; and pronouncing Ts like Ds – "You bedder believe it, baby."' Millions of cravat-wearers and shampoo-avoiders are now going to throw themselves under the wheels of oncoming express trains, or sign up to one of those sad incel websites.

How many first dates become second dates, and how many later dates become fully fledged relationships, before settling down into one of Suzana's 'situationships'? I haven't a clue, but so many people you see walking up or down your street are in couples, many of them pushing vast prams, so they must have started somewhere. My own bugbear, nurtured over several decades, is how many attractive, obviously interesting women go out with catastrophically daggy men. A woman I know with the most beautiful nose imaginable eventually gave in and got married to the startlingly dull management consultant who had been pursuing her for years, having started by merely stalking her. He has a face like a fish on a slab, and now their children do too. I have one friend who got so desperate she started going out with a Welshman. You bedder believe it, boyo.

23

Steam

My friend Peter came for dinner the other day. He's about the same age as me and he writes children's picture books for a living: he has done at least forty or fifty, possibly more (even he doesn't know exactly how many). 'What are you most afraid of?' I asked, opening the second bottle of red wine. 'Running out of steam,' he said. 'Ah,' said I.

This is, arguably, the BIG worry as we approach the age of sixty (but from which direction? as Kathy Lette once asked). We worry about our health and our children and (in my case) our chronic lack of funds, but the big one is steam, and the running out thereof. How many books have I left in me? How long before the quality begins to suffer, and how long before the ideas run out altogether? Peter says he is just finishing one up now, and soon he will have to go and sit in a nearby café with his notebook and laptop and wait for an idea to come. He doesn't have an idea for the next one yet, and he is hoping one will just ... appear, possibly out of a cup of coffee, possibly out of the lovely waitress, possibly out of the Danish pastry he is absently biting into. It will, I'm sure, because he is a p

The crucial thing is that he, the pro, isn't half as sure as I am. He's just hoping.

I know the book I am going to write next, or at least, I have an idea for one, but how much do I actually want to do it? Most of my books take between six months and a year to write, and this one would be quite heavy on research – never my favourite part of the journey. And having spent a while writing (and more often than not, not writing) this one, I feel exhausted, spent. But as always, I need the money, and you have to keep going. My friend David, who is much more productive than I (possibly because he writes both fiction and non-fiction), knows exactly what he will be writing for the next two to three years, and he has a fair idea of what he will be writing in five years' time, should he still be alive. The problem is not just dying early, before you can get all this work done. It's running out of steam, running out of ideas, running out of energy. One day, we all feel sure, the ideas will cease and we will no longer be writers. We will be retired, dead, former writers, however you want to put it. It's a terrifying prospect, and it seems to loom larger with every passing day.

I don't want to tread on the toes of the last book I published, *How to Be a Writer*, but the writing process has been much on my mind lately, as I edge warily towards the end of this book. This book is appreciably shorter than most of mine, and it may just be that I am finally learning concision, a good lesson to learn. (Essay subject: 'Most books are far too long, Discuss.') Or maybe my creativity is starting to fail. Maybe I am beginning to run out of steam.

My other friend David, who is a graphic designer, doesn't worry about running out of steam: the ideas keep coming, and when they don't, experience fills in for lost imagination. 'Do your clients know the difference?' I ask him. 'I'm not sure I do,' said he. These seem to me words of great wisdom.

How much steam is there left? We simply do not know. The problem is that any number of creative people have experienced a waning of their faculties as they have got older. I can think of several writers whose last few books were pretty feeble, and who had clearly been published because of past reliability rather than present performance. I think we should all accept that steam supplies are finite, and possibly even more finite than we imagine.

Jeremy Paxman has described this time as 'the lazy years, when no one will ask you to clean the gutters, for fear you will fall off the ladder and oblige them to spend hours hanging around A&E'. Perhaps we should embrace the finite nature of our steam supplies and do as little as possible. As I get older I feel that laziness has much to be said for it. We have all proved ourselves, and if we haven't, it's a bit late to try now. (For so many years, I considered myself to be 'promising'. I then seemed to segue straight into 'washed up' without any intervening stage of actual achievement. 'Pale, male and stale' was the way a couple of writer friends phrased it at a party, where we were all laying into the red wine as though there were limited supplies of that. Happily there were not.) Another writer friend has announced his intention to give up writing books, which he thinks is a thankless task, and reboot himself as a magician, or specifically, someone who teaches conjuring tricks to employees of City firms for oodles of money. I slightly envy him having a second string to his bow. I am terribly good at going out to lunch, but not much else. I can walk up to the end of the road to buy a Crunchie, but there's very little call for such once-valued skills in the marketplace these days. To be fair, though, I have come to despise the marketplace, which rewards suits and middlemen far more than people who actually do things, or make things. I know a guy in Cornwall who makes, and repairs, ancient stringed instruments to an incredibly high standard. He is an artist. He should be rich. He is not.

Because time is so precious, and because steam supplies are so limited, we have to make the most of what we have. In 2011 an Australian nurse called Bronnie Ware, who specialised in end-of-life care, published a book called *The Top Five Regrets of the Dying*. Number one was this: 'I wish I'd had the courage to live a life true to myself, not the life others expected of me.' In other words: regrets, I've had a few. It's the clarity of oncoming death that seems to crystallise these thoughts. I'd rather have that clarity now, right now, while I can still walk unaided and don't need to suck my dinner through a straw.*

But sooner or later, as sure as eggs is eggs, we shall run out of steam, and when it happens, we should just accept it and retire gracefully. My armchair is waiting. My cup of tea sits beside me. There are biscuits in the kitchen, and a multi-pack of Toffee Crisps in my chocolate stash. All is ready for (I hope) many years of doing very little indeed. When Jim

---

* In April 2022, *Saga Magazine* commissioned a survey on its readers' main regrets in life. Number 1 was 'Spending too much time worrying'. Number 2 was 'Not working harder at school' (now that ship really has sailed). Number 3 was 'Marrying the wrong person'. Number 4 was 'Not spending more time with family'. And number 5 was 'Not keeping in touch with friends more'. 'Not taking more risks' was seventh, and 'Spending too much time trying to please others' was eighth. Twenty-four per cent of respondents said they regretted nothing, but I'm not sure we quite believe them, do we, readers?

Hacker became prime minister in *Yes, Prime Minister*, he asked his senior civil servant, Sir Humphrey Appleby, what he was supposed to do with the job. Sir Humphrey told him that there were many things he *could* do, and a few things he probably *ought* to do, but very few things that he *had* to do. Sir Humphrey recommended a course of 'masterly inactivity'. Sounds like the future for me.

Unless another brilliant idea for a book emerges in a coffee shop. Or a pub. (I once thought of an idea for a book in a pub. I wrote it, and it became by far my lowest-selling book. Forget pubs then.)

24

Happy?

This, of course, is the nub, the destination, where this book was always going to go. Are we happy? Is our life enough? Are we enough?

I am, at heart, an optimist, and my optimism has been well tested over the years. According to Ian Sample in the *Guardian*, 'People who have a rosy outlook on the world may live healthier, longer lives because they have fewer stressful events to cope with.' Scientists, whoever they may be, established that while optimists reacted to stressful situations in much the same way as pessimists, they generally fared better because they didn't have so many stressful events in their lives.

How do optimists do this? It turns out that they steer clear of arguments, they don't lose their keys and they don't leave their umbrellas on the bus. Or if they do either of the latter two, they don't let it ruin their day. It's perceiving things as stressful that actually makes them stressful. 'If you can keep your head when all about you are losing theirs and blaming it on you,' as Kipling wrote, then you'll be happier and, it turns out, healthier too. For having a glass-half-full attitude is believed to contribute to healthy ageing, although as yet researchers haven't a clue why.

In other words, mellow is better than mad, and gammons need to loosen up. (Possibly eat and drink a little less, too.)

My optimism is often sorely stretched. When I am recording *Round Britain Quiz*, my quiz partner Paul Sinha and I always expect the worst: questions we won't be able to answer, that everyone else listening will know and which will leave us completely stumped. It has happened before, and it will happen again, for sure. Everyone else (including the producer and our rival teams) has far higher expectations of us than we do.

But this is a tiny oasis of pessimism in a desert of optimism. Probably better considered the other way round: an island of pessimism in an ocean of optimism. No, this metaphor isn't working at all.

For otherwise I am a proud optimist. I try to see the best in everyone, until the day comes when they prove that there's no best to be had and what they have to offer to everyone is distinctly sub-par. I don't obsess about illness or death, figuring that when they come after me, there will be very little I can do about it. And when I have been completely on my financial uppers, I have always had something in reserve, something that will come up, a half-forgotten payment that will come in from somewhere and save my bacon. Is it a nice day now? Then it might be a nice day later as well. Is it raining? Well, you never know, it might stop.

I have been reading a very odd book indeed, written by a young entrepreneur named Steven Bartlett, with the very slightly off-putting title *Happy Sexy Millionaire*. (The words 'fuck off' come to mind.) Although he is sometimes a bit of a dick, he has some impressive and interesting insights into the modern world, and particularly on the way social media distorts people's values and expectations. 'Maybe you've always been happy, but the world, social media and external comparisons have convinced you that you can't possibly be.' I went for a drink the other day with four friends from my schooldays, three women and a man: we usually meet up every couple of months and go to the same slightly unsatisfactory pub a couple of miles from my home. One of the women, who has just retired after a long and eminent career as an obs and gynae consultant, announced that her secret to happiness was to eschew all social media, permanently. She has a Facebook account (which she never uses), but nothing on Twitter or Instagram, and although she is a member of a WhatsApp group, it's only with the rest of us to arrange these occasional drinks.* She has recently dyed the right side of her hair pink, which I think all newly retired people should seriously consider.

The philosopher Lao Tzu said that much of our happiness could be attained just by detaching ourselves from a destination mindset, that living too much in the past or future just makes us miserable. 'A good traveller has no fixed plans and is not intent on arriving,' he wrote, which I'm afraid is the opposite of me in airports. Dying your hair pink on retiring seems to me part of the journey rather than the destination, celebrating the fact that there is life after work. According to Bartlett, 'this is one of the great paradoxes of happiness:

---

* I am not a member of the WhatsApp group as I don't have a mobile phone: I have to be contacted separately when a drink is in the offing. Indeed, if I'm going to be honest, I'm not sure I know what a WhatsApp group actually is.

you have to call off the search in order to find everything you have been searching for'. He talked to the transformational therapist Marisa Peer, who told him, 'In thirty-three years of being a therapist, I've worked with everyone from long-suffering movie stars to anxious Olympic athletes to depressed schoolteachers, and they all have the same problem: they almost always don't believe they're enough. I've worked with thousands of drug addicts and I've never met one that thought they were enough.'

Well, I'm enough, and so are you. (The fact that you bought this book and read this far proves it, as far as I am concerned.)

I think that when you reach this age you know who you are and you don't really care any more what anyone thinks of you. (That would be the ideal situation, anyway.) Unlike lots of young people.

Bartlett mentions a plastic surgeon whose business is booming, and who says that 'over one-third of his clients come to him with visual references of social media influencers they want to look like, i.e. they bring a screenshot of a fake, filtered person and ask him to make them as unrealistic so they can show their followers and continue the cycle of toxic comparisons'. This is lunacy. Look in the mirror, see a drastically imperfect body and think, well, it'll do, because it will.

At the age of just eighteen, the influencer and multi-millionaire Kylie Jenner had the word 'sanity' tattooed on her hip. She did it because 'I felt a little bit like I was going insane. Or, I was going to.' So she had a word tattooed on her hip so that every time she saw it she reminded herself that it was not time to go doolally, that she had a brand to nurture and money to make, and that straitjackets and padded cells are a less-than-good look. Kylie Jenner is followed by more than 300 million people on Instagram. That's more than me (46) and less than only Cristiano Ronaldo (388 million). Bartlett describes following her as 'voluntary mental self-harm on an enormous scale. You wouldn't continue to read books that told you you're a worthless, ugly, unsuccessful piece of shit, so why have you chosen to fill a digital library with content that will evidently do the same?'

This is not a question we need worry too much about, because I am guessing that only a tiny percentage of people who read this book will follow Kylie Jenner on Instagram. But it's impossible to overestimate how important it is to one's mental health and general serenity that you like, even love, yourself. As Whitney Houston once warbled, 'Learning to love yourself is the greatest love of all.' If she had listened to the song she sang, she might not have accidentally drowned herself in a hotel bathtub after ingesting epic quantities of cocaine.

Bartlett has lots of good advice for all this. 'If a person could do only *one* simple thing to increase their health and happiness then expressing gratitude on a regular basis must be it.' I have been banging on about this for years. Thanking everyone for everything makes them feel good but also makes you feel good. In my dotage I have become almost absurdly courteous. The alternative is to throw your weight around like a normal-sized John Bercow, bullying the world and shouting at everyone and generally spreading misery and hatred rather than sweetness and light. It has worked for bullies, tyrants and sociopaths down the ages, until the time when karma comes to call, and you have to jump off your yacht into the briny to avoid jail. Can you imagine how terrible it must have been to actually BE Robert Maxwell? Possibly even worse, I would say, than being John Bercow.

'Are you happy?' I asked my old friends at one of our WALLS lunches. 'Right now, very,' said David, tucking into his third pint of Estrella. The consensus was that while there were bad moments, bad hours and bad days, this was quite a good time to be about sixty, healthy and reasonably well off, as most of them are. Long lunches with friends can only be a good thing, even if we talk endlessly about our aches and pains and demented parents. And rolling home feeling merry at half-past five is definitely an improvement on going back to work and snoozing at your desk. My feeling is that, for all the fears of the future, these are in some ways the best years of our lives. Ambition gone, children grown, long walks easily available, pubs and restaurants open and absolutely no need to go to the theatre if you don't want to: I'm not sure I see any downsides, except those that are undoubtedly to come. Live in the present, take nothing for granted and never, ever watch daytime TV – unless you feel like it, of course. Rules for life that make complete sense to me, as a fully paid-up member of the young/old.

25

News Update III

The cull continues. Polly's best friend L's mad old father was given two weeks to live and died two days later. My old friend J's elder sister's cancer came back and she's now lying in a hospital in Barnet receiving palliative care only. She's just sixty-six. I saw her at a birthday party no more than three years ago and she was in typically robust, argumentative form.* My friend C's younger brother died of a massive heart attack in his sleep, aged fifty-five, and a few weeks later their father died in his early nineties of complications from Alzheimer's. Eighteen months ago C's mother, father and brother were all still alive and apparently healthy; now, having had no children, he is the last of his line. My mother has a friend in her forties who has been diagnosed with breast cancer, and who, as well as all the normal treatments, has adopted a radical sugar-free diet and thinks my mother should do the same. 'I'm ninety-one,' says my mother, 'and as far as I'm concerned, a life without cake is a life not worth

---

* She died a week after this was written.

living.' My father has just turned ninety-one and is now frail and rumoured to be on his last legs. Bollocks to rumours: I feel sure he will outlive us all, the old bastard.*

Does it feel as though everyone is ill or dying? Sometimes, yes, and right now, definitely. But most of us young/oldies are muddling along all right and will do so for several years to come, with a following wind. I think it's just that as we get older, the illness and death of others becomes a much bigger part of our lives. We already go to more funerals than weddings, and there's an argument that as you get older, funerals become more fun than weddings, and certainly much cheaper. There's no awful stag night for a funeral, there's no need to buy a present for the deceased, and if you just don't fancy it on the day, you simply don't have to go. The worst funerals I ever went to have been for young people, the absolute worst being for my friend Esther, previously mentioned, who died of a brain tumour in 2003, aged forty-four. Her two small daughters were there, and the mood wasn't so much sombre as terrifyingly bleak. There was no sense of celebration for her life; there was just crippling, terrible sadness at the early snuffing-out of this vibrant, wonderful person we all loved. The funerals I have been to since have at least had a sense of a life well lived, and have remembered the departed with fondness, even with humour, but not this one. Her grandparents were there, for fuck's sake.

Nowadays, when someone of my generation or my parents' generation breathes their last, there *is* a sense of a life well lived, and even if no one actually says the words 'he/she had a good innings', everyone is certainly thinking it. But as my

---

* He is still alive, several months later.

son said, after getting out for a golden duck last weekend, 'I'd almost rather get out for a golden duck than make 15 or 20. Because if you make 15 or 20, you should really have got 30, and if you get 30 you really should have got 50, and if you get 50 you really should have made 100 ... ' and on and on it goes. Some lives naturally come to an end; others are rudely abbreviated. My mother's only remaining ambition, she says, is to outlive my father, a mere forty-seven years after they got divorced. And he has apparently just married the Polish former au pair girl he ran off with, to the local Holiday Inn, in 1974. What an old romantic.

Death is all around us, but life goes on, I'm glad to say. In my dotage I have become a creature of habit, doing the same things over and over and over again and extracting quite a lot of pleasure from this. It drives Polly mad, the way I make a pot of tea at between 3.45 and 4 in the afternoon and ask her if she wants a cup. When even your courtesy drives your partner mad, you know you are well suited.

Happiness, I have concluded, is all about simplicity. Keep life simple and happiness will follow. I met a bloke at a party yesterday, an opera director, about the same age as me, who said that he is constantly shuttling between the twin poles of anxiety and dread. Dread? I wondered. But he is an opera director, constantly having to do difficult things with difficult people, whereas I am just a writer, sitting in my bedroom, more often than not in my dressing gown, laptop on lap, avoiding the outside world if at all possible. I have excised dread from my life by not doing all the things that I used to that I had come to dread. Even my anxiety, which is usually about money, isn't what it was. Funnily enough, the opera director also said that he was giving up directing opera. He had been doing it for forty years and he had other things to do. He told me some of them and they all sounded incredibly ambitious and energy-consuming. I wanted to tell him just to scale back and do less, but I was distracted, possibly by a bottle of decent wine I had spotted in the fridge, so I didn't get the opportunity.

The last word, as so often in life, goes to my mum. My daughter was chatting to her about something, and my mum referred to someone they both knew as 'an old cunt'. My daughter was taken aback, having never heard her use the word before. So was I when she told me, as I hadn't either. My mother was unrepentant. 'I'm old,' she said, 'and I can do what I like.' She's right: she can; and so, I think, can we.

Acknowledgements

Cliff Allen, John Ash, James Berkmann, Martha Berkmann, Jean Berkmann-Barwis, Richard Beswick, Paula Bingham, Joanna Briscoe, Chris Carter, Thomas Coops, Richard Corden, Amanda Craig, Matthew Greenburgh, Zoe Gullen, Sarah Hesketh, Ian Hislop, Richard Ingrams (for the title), Mark Jacobs, David Jaques, Bob Jones, Aalia Khan, Roz Levine, Nick Lezard, Paul McAstocker, Howard McMinn, Mark Mason, Meg Meagher, Alex Monroe, John Mullan, Nick Newman, Julian Parker, Francis Peckham, Susy Pote, Neal Ransome, Lucy Reese, Gavin Rodgers, Terence Russoff, Kate Saunders, Martin Stubbs, David 'D.J.' Taylor, Russell Taylor, Sam Taylor, Pat Thomas, Bethen Thorpe, Jane Thynne, Patrick Walsh, Nathalie Webb, Helen White, Adrian Williamson, John Woolman, Jason Wright, 'Swiss' Tony Zucker.

Credits

1   Nick Cave, The Red Hand Files, issue #153, June 2021, theredhandfiles.com

47   'Phenomenal facial hair: are you ready for the circle beard and double moustache?', *Guardian*, 8 July 2021

47*   'Stayin' Alive', lyrics by Barry Alan Gibb, Maurice Ernest Gibb and Robin Hugh Gibb. Lyrics © Universal Music Publishing Group, Warner Chappell Music, Inc

53*   @thewritertype via Twitter, 18 June 2021

109*   Douglas Adams, 'Build It and We Will Come', *Independent on Sunday*, November 1999, in *The Salmon of Doubt: Hitchhiking the Galaxy One Last Time* (London: William Heinemann, 2002)

133   'Does Your Mother Know', lyrics by Benny Andersson and Bjorn K. Ulvaeus. Lyrics © Universal/Union Songs Musikforlag AB

136*   @amaditalks via Twitter, 21 October 2019

141   Simon Cowell, quoted in *Glamour*, April 2008

146   Author photo: © Sophie Baker / skull: pattang/
         Shutterstock

169   Renata Salecl, *The Tyranny of Choice* (London:
         Profile, 2011)

170   Barry Schwartz, 'The Paradox of Choice', TED
         Talk, July 2005

193–4   Justin Myers, 'Arrives late, pours your wine
         and eats onions – 56 dating red flags that
         should send you running', *Guardian*, 15
         October 2022

198   Bronnie Ware, *The Top Five Regrets of the
         Dying: A Life Transformed by the Dearly
         Departing* (Alexandria: Balboa Press, 2011)

201   Ian Sample, 'Reasons to be cheerful:
         optimists live longer, says study', *Guardian*, 7
         March 2022

203–4,   Steven Bartlett, *Happy Sexy Millionaire*
205   (London: Yellow Kite, 2021)

204   'Kylie Reveals All', *V Magazine*, 2017

205   'Greatest Love of All' by Linda Creed and
         Michael Masser. Lyrics © EMI Golden Torch
         Music Corp., EMI Gold Horizon Music Corp.